W9-CDP-260

All proceeds
from the sale of this booklet
will be contributed to
The National Book Foundation.

The National Book Foundation

The National Book Awards

Forty-eight Years of Literary Excellence

Winners and Finalists
1950 - 1997

The Board of Directors of The National Book Foundation
would like to thank:

Random House, Inc.
Ellen Reed, production manager
Virginia Avery, copy editor
Martha Schwartz, copy chief
Carole Lowenstein, designer
Andy Carpenter, art director

Text paper donated by Random House, Inc.

ComCom, Division of R.R. Donnelly & Sons (text composition)
Linda Friedman, customer service representative
Carolyn Johnson, programmer

Quebecor Printing/Martinsburg (text printing and binding)
Sally Warner, customer service representative

Coral Graphic Services, Inc. (cover printing and paper)
Frank V. Cappo, president

Ingram Book Group (promotion, order fulfillment and distribution)
Michael F. Lovett, president & CEO

ISBN 1-889099-24-4

Cover art: *Pomona Britannica*, by George Brookshaw, London, 1817.
Courtesy of Rare Books Division,
The New York Public Library, Astor,
Lenox & Tilden Foundations

For more information about the annual
National Book Awards competition and the programs of
The National Book Foundation presenting National Book Award
winners and finalists in communities across the country,
please contact:

The National Book Foundation
260 Fifth Avenue, 9th floor
New York, N.Y. 10001
phone: 212-685-0261
fax: 212-213-6570

The National Book Awards
and The National Book Foundation:
Honoring an American Literary Tradition

In the spring of 1989, as The National Book Awards moved toward the completion of their fourth decade, the Board of Directors determined that the time had come to broaden the scope of the organization beyond the single focus of literary recognition.

The prestigious Award would be even further burnished, its cachet enriched, by strengthening its cultural context to involve the creation of programs that would complement the conferring of awards.

As a result, The National Book Awards now serve as a centerpiece for programs featuring Award Winners and Finalists. The National Book Foundation raises funds to support literary programs around the country in which authors talk about their work and give readings. These authors provide personal insights into their creativity, in the process revealing secrets of the writing life—parting the veil on a mysterious process. Or they discover the pleasures of reading, tracing the roots of their literary development to books that had served as their personal, primary sources, and to which they turn for inspiration.

The National Book Foundation came into being at a time of deepening concern about literacy in America. Recognizing that the problems of reading and writing exist across a complex spectrum of knowledge—not only among those who do not possess skills, but equally among those who can read but do not—the Board has directed its energies toward "literate literacy."

The Foundation is in an ideal position to become an activist force bringing living exemplars of quality writing before a pluralistic public.

The mainstay for The National Book Awards has been and will continue to be the publishing industry at all points in its varied spectrum, from small presses to multinational corporations. The Foundation is also forging public–private partnerships with government agencies, foundations, and individuals who know that books can make a difference.

The National Book Awards were created nearly one-half century ago during a period when books suffered less competition in the culture at large. More books are published now, but fewer people seem to be reading. We live in a paradoxical and uncertain era; a book should represent more than ever a source of refuge, a voice of reason and inspiration in an increasingly distracting world.

The National Book Foundation seeks to ennoble that voice, and it is in the spirit of preserving an American literary tradition that we offer this booklet—a roster that speaks eloquently of the forceful and unique role of American writing in our culture.

NEIL BALDWIN
Executive Director
March 1998

THE NATIONAL BOOK AWARDS

A Key to the Symbols

*WINNER
+SPECIAL CITATION
NO SYMBOL INDICATES A NOMINEE/FINALIST

1950
(Nominees not Announced)

Fiction

*Nelson Algren—THE MAN WITH THE GOLDEN ARM

Nonfiction

*Ralph L. Rusk—RALPH WALDO EMERSON
+Lincoln Barnett—THE UNIVERSE AND DR. EINSTEIN
+H. A. Overstreet—THE MATURE MIND
+Eleanor Roosevelt—THIS I REMEMBER
+Lillian Smith—KILLERS OF THE DREAM
+Kenneth P. Williams—LINCOLN FINDS A GENERAL

Poetry

*William Carlos Williams—PATERSON: BOOK III and SELECTED POEMS

1951
(Nominees Not Announced)

Fiction

*William Faulkner—THE COLLECTED STORIES OF WILLIAM FAULKNER
+Brendan Gill—THE TROUBLE OF ONE HOUSE

Nonfiction

*Newton Arvin—HERMAN MELVILLE

Poetry

*Wallace Stevens—THE AURORAS OF AUTUMN

Fiction

*James Jones—FROM HERE TO ETERNITY
James Agee—THE MORNING WATCH
Truman Capote—THE GRASS HARP
William Faulkner—REQUIEM FOR A NUN
Caroline Gordon—THE STRANGE CHILDREN
Thomas Mann—THE HOLY SINNER
John P. Marquand—MELVILLE GOODWIN USA
J. D. Salinger—THE CATCHER IN THE RYE
William Styron—LIE DOWN IN DARKNESS
Jessamyn West—THE WITCH DIGGERS
Herman Wouk—THE CAINE MUTINY

Nonfiction

*Rachel Carson—THE SEA AROUND US
Hannah Arendt—THE ORIGINS OF TOTALITARIANISM
Marshall Davidson—LIFE IN AMERICA
F. W. Dupee—HENRY JAMES
Waldo Frank—BIRTH OF A WORLD
Douglas S. Freeman—GEORGE WASHINGTON
Erich Fromm—THE FORGOTTEN LANGUAGE
Oscar Handlin—THE UPROOTED
Alfred Kazin—A WALKER IN THE CITY
Dumas Malone—JEFFERSON AND THE RIGHTS OF MAN
C. Wright Mills—WHITE COLLAR
Arthur Mizener—THE FAR SIDE OF PARADISE
Lewis Mumford—CONDUCT OF LIFE
Merlo Pusey—CHARLES EVANS HUGHES
Nathan Schachner—THOMAS JEFFERSON
William Carlos Williams—THE AUTOBIOGRAPHY OF WILLIAM CARLOS
  WILLIAMS
C. Vann Woodward—REUNION AND REACTION

Poetry

*Marianne Moore—COLLECTED POEMS
W. H. Auden—NONES
William Rose Benét—THE SPIRIT OF THE SCENE
Richard Eberhart—SELECTED POEMS
Horace Gregory—SELECTED POEMS OF HORACE GREGORY
Randall Jarrell—THE SEVEN-LEAGUE CRUTCHES
Theodore Roethke—PRAISE TO THE END
Muriel Rukeyser—SELECTED POEMS
William Carlos Williams—COLLECTED EARLIER POEMS
William Carlos Williams—PATERSON: BOOK IV

Fiction

*Ralph Ellison—INVISIBLE MAN
    Isabel Bolton—MANY MANSIONS
    H. L. Davis—WINDS OF MORNING
    Thomas Gallagher—THE GATHERING DARKNESS
    Ernest Hemingway—THE OLD MAN AND THE SEA
    Carl Jones—JEFFERSON SELLECK
    Peter Martin—THE LANDSMAN
    May Sarton—A SHOWER OF SUMMER DAYS
    Jean Stafford—THE GATHERING WHEEL
    John Steinbeck—EAST OF EDEN
    William Carlos Williams—THE BUILD-UP

Nonfiction

*Bernard A. De Voto—THE COURSE OF AN EMPIRE
    Herbert Agar—A DECLARATION OF FAITH
    Conrad Aiken—USHANT
    Frederick L. Allen—THE BIG CHANGE
    Robert Brittain—LET THERE BE BREAD
    Van Wyck Brooks—THE CONFIDENT YEARS
    Whittaker Chambers—WITNESS
    Eleanor Clark—ROME AND A VILLA
    William O. Douglas—BEYOND THE HIGH HIMALAYAS
    Douglas S. Freeman—GEORGE WASHINGTON, VOL. V
    Eric Goldman—RENDEZVOUS WITH DESTINY
    Learned Hand—THE SPIRIT OF LIBERTY
    Irving Howe—WILLIAM FAULKNER
    Herbert Muller—THE USES OF THE PAST
    F. S. C. Northrup—THE TAMING OF THE NATIONS
    Katherine Anne Porter—THE DAYS BEFORE
    J. G. Randall—MIDSTREAM: LINCOLN THE PRESIDENT
    Benjamin Thomas—ABRAHAM LINCOLN
    Dixon Wecter—SAM CLEMENS OF HANNIBAL
    Kenneth P. Williams—LINCOLN FINDS A GENERAL, VOL. III
    Edmund Wilson—THE SHORES OF LIGHT

Poetry

*Archibald MacLeish—COLLECTED POEMS, 1917–1952
    Stanley Burnshaw—EARLY AND LATE TESTAMENT
    Thomas H. Ferril—NEW AND SELECTED POEMS
    Robert Hillyer—THE SUBURB BY THE SEA
    Ernest Kroll—CAPE HORN AND OTHER POEMS
    W. S. Merwin—A MASK FOR JANUS

Byron H. Reece—A SONG OF JOY
Naomi Replansky—RING SONG
Kenneth Rexroth—THE DRAGON AND THE UNICORN
Jesse Stuart—KENTUCKY IS MY LAND
Ridgely Torrence—POEMS
Peter Viereck—THE FIRST MORNING

1954
(Nominees not Announced)

Fiction

*Saul Bellow—THE ADVENTURES OF AUGIE MARCH

Nonfiction

*Bruce Catton—A STILLNESS AT APPOMATTOX

Poetry

*Conrad Aiken—COLLECTED POEMS

1955

Fiction

*William Faulkner—A FABLE
    Harriet Arnow—THE DOLLMAKER
    Hamilton Basso—THE VIEW FROM POMPEY'S HEAD
    Davis Grubb—THE NIGHT OF THE HUNTER
    Randall Jarrell—PICTURES FROM AN INSTITUTION
    Milton Lott—THE LAST HUNT
    Frederick Manfred—LORD GRIZZLY
    William March—THE BAD SEED
    Wright Morris—THE HUGE SEASON
    Frank Rooney—THE COURTS OF MEMORY
    John Steinbeck—SWEET THURSDAY

Nonfiction

*Joseph Wood Krutch—THE MEASURE OF MAN
    Van Wyck Brooks—SCENES AND PORTRAITS
    Harrison Brown—THE CHALLENGE OF MAN'S FUTURE

Elmer Davis—BUT WE WERE BORN FREE
Hermann Hagedorn—THE ROOSEVELT FAMILY OF SAGAMORE HILL
Paul Horgan—GREAT RIVER
John La Farge—THE MANNER IS ORDINARY
David Lavender—BENT'S FORT
Carl Sandburg—ABRAHAM LINCOLN
Wallace Stegner—BEYOND THE HUNDREDTH MERIDIAN
Norman Thomas—THE TEST OF FREEDOM
E. B. White—THE SECOND TREE FROM THE CORNER

Poetry

*Wallace Stevens—THE COLLECTED POEMS OF WALLACE STEVENS
+e. e. cummings—POEMS, 1923–1954
Leonie Adams—POEMS: A COLLECTION
Louise Bogan—COLLECTED POEMS, 1923–1953
Robinson Jeffers—HUNGERFIELD AND OTHER POEMS
Archibald MacLeish—SONGS FOR EVE
Phyllis McGinley—THE LOVE LETTERS OF PHYLLIS MCGINLEY
Merrill Moore—THE VERSE DIARY OF A PSYCHIATRIST
LeRoy Smith—A CHARACTER INVENTED
May Swenson—Poems in POETS OF TODAY
William Carlos Williams—THE DESERT MUSIC AND OTHER POEMS
Marya Zaturenska—SELECTED POEMS

————————— **1956** —————————

Fiction

*John O'Hara—TEN NORTH FREDERICK
Paul Bowles—THE SPIDER'S HOUSE
Shirley Ann Grau—THE BLACK PRINCE
MacKinlay Kantor—ANDERSONVILLE
Flannery O'Connor—A GOOD MAN IS HARD TO FIND
May Sarton—FAITHFUL ARE THE WOUNDS
Robert Penn Warren—BAND OF ANGELS
Eudora Welty—THE BRIDE OF THE INNISFALLEN
Herman Wouk—MARJORIE MORNINGSTAR

Nonfiction

*Herbert Kubly—AN AMERICAN IN ITALY
Gay Wilson Allen—THE SOLITARY SINGER
Alan Barth—GOVERNMENT BY INVESTIGATION
Rachel Carson—THE EDGE OF THE SEA
Clifford Dowdey—THE LAND THEY FOUGHT FOR

John Gunther—INSIDE AFRICA
Richard Hofstadter—THE AGE OF REFORM
Murray Kempton—PART OF OUR TIME
Anne Morrow Lindbergh—GIFT FROM THE SEA
Milton Mayer—THEY THOUGHT THEY WERE FREE
Allan Temko—NOTRE DAME OF PARIS
Harry S. Truman—YEAR OF DECISIONS
Edmund Wilson—THE SCROLLS FROM THE DEAD SEA

Poetry

*W. H. Auden—THE SHIELD OF ACHILLES
Elizabeth Bishop—POEMS, NORTH AND SOUTH
John Ciardi—AS IF
Isabella Gardner—BIRTHDAYS FROM THE OCEAN
Donald Hall—EXILES AND MARRIAGES
Randall Jarrell—SELECTED POEMS
Adrienne Rich—THE DIAMOND CUTTERS
William Carlos Williams—JOURNEY TO LOVE

1957

Fiction

*Wright Morris—THE FIELD OF VISION
Nelson Algren—WALK ON THE WILD SIDE
James Baldwin—GIOVANNI'S ROOM
Saul Bellow—SEIZE THE DAY
B. J. Chute—GREENWILLOW
A. B. Guthrie—THESE THOUSAND YEARS
John Hersey—A SINGLE PEBBLE
John Hunt—GENERATIONS OF MEN
Edwin O'Connor—THE LAST HURRAH
J. F. Powers—THE PRESENCE OF GRACE
Elizabeth Spencer—THE VOICE AT THE BACK DOOR
James Thurber—FURTHER FABLES FOR OUR TIME

Nonfiction

*George F. Kennan—RUSSIA LEAVES THE WAR
Samuel F. Bemis—JOHN QUINCY ADAMS AND THE UNION
James MacGregor Burns—ROOSEVELT: THE LION AND THE FOX
Bruce Catton—THIS HALLOWED GROUND
William Chambers—OLD BULLION BENTON
Stuart Chase—GUIDES TO STRAIGHT THINKING
Arthur H. Compton—THE ATOMIC QUEST

Frank Freidel—FRANKLIN D. ROOSEVELT: THE TRIUMPH
Eric Goldman—THE CRUCIAL DECADE
Kathryn Hulme—THE NUN'S STORY
Paul Murray Kendall—RICHARD III
John F. Kennedy—PROFILES IN COURAGE
Samuel Lubell—THE REVOLT OF THE MODERATES
Perry Miller—THE RAVEN AND THE WHALE
Lewis Mumford—TRANSFORMATIONS OF MAN
Edwin W. Teale—AUTUMN ACROSS AMERICA
Robert Penn Warren—SEGREGATION
William Whyte, Jr.—THE ORGANIZATION MAN

Poetry

*Richard Wilbur—THINGS OF THIS WORLD
Edgar Bowers—THE FORM OF LOSS
Leah B. Drake—THIS TILTING DUST
Charles E. Eaton—GREENHOUSE IN THE GARDEN
Kenneth Fearing—NEW AND SELECTED POEMS
Robert Fitzgerald—IN THE ROSE OF TIME
Katherine Haskins—VILLA NARCISSE
Rolfe Humphries—GREEN ARMOR ON GREEN GROUND
Joseph Langland—Poems in POEMS OF TODAY, III
Anne Morrow Lindbergh—THE UNICORN
W. S. Merwin—GREEN WITH BEASTS
Marianne Moore—LIKE A BULWARK
Ezra Pound—SECTION: ROCK DRILL
Kenneth Rexroth—IN DEFENSE OF THE EARTH
John Hall Wheelock—POEMS OLD AND NEW

1958

Fiction

*John Cheever—THE WAPSHOT CHRONICLE
James Agee—A DEATH IN THE FAMILY
James Gould Cozzens—BY LOVE POSSESSED
Mark Harris—SOMETHING ABOUT A SOLDIER
Andrew Lytle—THE VELVET HORN
Bernard Malamud—THE ASSISTANT
Wright Morris—LOVE AMONG THE CANNIBALS
Vladimir Nabokov—PNIN
Ayn Rand—ATLAS SHRUGGED
Nancy Wilson Ross—THE RETURN OF LADY BRACE
May Sarton—THE BIRTH OF A GRANDFATHER

Nonfiction

*Catherine Drinker Bowen—THE LION AND THE THRONE
    Margaret Coit—MR. BARUCH
    Will Durant—THE REFORMATION
    Louis Hacker—ALEXANDER HAMILTON IN THE AMERICAN TRADITION
    Gilbert Highet—POETS IN A LANDSCAPE
    Mark deWolfe Howe—JUSTICE HOLMES: THE SHAPING YEARS, 1841–1870
    Henry A. Kissinger—NUCLEAR WEAPONS AND FOREIGN POLICY
    Mary McCarthy—MEMORIES OF A CATHOLIC GIRLHOOD
    Max F. Milliken & W. W. Rostow—A PROPOSAL: KEY TO AN EFFECTIVE
      FOREIGN POLICY
    Vance Packard—THE HIDDEN PERSUADERS
    John Pullen—THE TWENTIETH MAINE
    David Schoenbrun—AS FRANCE GOES
    Gwen Terasaki—BRIDGE TO THE SUN
    W. S. White—THE CITADEL

Poetry

*Robert Penn Warren—PROMISES: POEMS, 1954–1956
    Daniel Berrigan—TIME WITHOUT NUMBER
    Philip Booth—LETTER FROM A DISTANT LAND
    Edwin G. Burrows—THE ARCTIC TERN
    H. D. (Hilda Doolittle)—SELECTED POEMS OF H. D.
    Richard Eberhart—GREAT PRAISES
    Richmond Lattimore—POEMS
    Howard Moss—SWIMMER IN THE AIR
    May Sarton—IN TIME LIKE AIR
    Eli Siegel—HOT AFTERNOONS HAVE BEEN IN MONTANA
    William Jay Smith—POEMS: 1947–1957
    Wallace Stevens—OPUS POSTHUMOUS
    James Wright—THE GREEN WALL

1959

Fiction

*Bernard Malamud—THE MAGIC BARREL
    J. P. Donleavy—THE GINGER MAN
    William Humphrey—HOME FROM THE HILL
    Vladimir Nabokov—LOLITA
    John O'Hara—FROM THE TERRACE
    J. R. Salamanca—THE LOST COUNTRY
    Anya Seton—THE WINTHROP WOMAN
    Robert Travers—ANATOMY OF A MURDER

Nonfiction

*J. Christopher Herold—MISTRESS TO AN AGE: A LIFE OF MADAME DE STAËL
   Hannah Arendt—THE HUMAN CONDITION
   Lester Atwell—PRIVATE
   Daniel J. Boorstin—THE AMERICANS
   Anne Braden—THE WALL BETWEEN
   Charles Ferguson—NAKED TO MINE ENEMIES
   Shelby Foote—THE CIVIL WAR, VOL. I
   John Kenneth Galbraith—THE AFFLUENT SOCIETY
   Harry Golden—ONLY IN AMERICA
   George F. Kennan—RUSSIA, THE ATOM AND THE WEST
   Louis Kronenberger—MARLBOROUGH'S DUCHESS
   Flora Lewis—A CASE HISTORY OF HOPE
   Edgar Snow—JOURNEY TO THE BEGINNINGS

Poetry

*Theodore Roethke—WORDS FOR THE WIND
   John Ciardi—I MARRY YOU
   e. e. cummings—POEMS
   Archibald MacLeish—J. B.
   Howard Nemerov—MIRRORS AND WINDOWS
   Karl Shapiro—POEMS FOR A JEW
   May Swenson—A CAGE OF SPINES
   William Carlos Williams—PATERSON, BOOK IV

1960

Fiction

*Philip Roth—GOODBYE, COLUMBUS
   Louis Auchincloss—PURSUIT OF THE PRODIGAL
   Hamilton Basso—THE LIGHT INFANTRY BALL
   Saul Bellow—HENDERSON THE RAIN KING
   Evan S. Connell, Jr.—MRS. BRIDGE
   William Faulkner—THE MANSION
   Mark Harris—WAKE UP, STUPID
   John Hersey—THE WAR LOVER
   H. L. Humes—MEN DIE
   Shirley Jackson—THE HAUNTING OF HILL HOUSE
   Elizabeth Janeway—THE THIRD CHOICE
   James Jones—THE PISTOL
   Warren Miller—THE COOL WORLD
   James Purdy—MALCOLM
   Leo Rosten—THE RETURN OF H*Y*M*A*N* K*A*P*L*A*N*

John Updike—THE POORHOUSE FAIR
Robert Penn Warren—THE CAVE
Morris West—THE DEVIL'S ADVOCATE

Nonfiction

*Richard Ellmann—JAMES JOYCE
Jacques Barzun—THE HOUSE OF INTELLECT
A. A. Berle—POWER WITHOUT PROPERTY
Croswell Bowen—THE CURSE OF THE MISBEGOTTEN
Douglass Cater—THE FOURTH BRANCH OF GOVERNMENT
Marchette Chute—TWO GENTLE MEN
A. Hunter Dupree—ASA GRAY
Tyrone Guthrie—LIFE IN THE THEATRE
Alan Harrington—LIFE IN THE CRYSTAL PALACE
Moss Hart—ACT ONE
Howard Mumford Jones—ONE GREAT SOCIETY
Ward Jones—THE GREAT COMMAND
Matthew Josephson—EDISON
Joseph Wood Krutch—HUMAN NATURE AND THE HUMAN CONDITION
Alfred Lansing—ENDURANCE
Margaret Leech—IN THE DAYS OF WILLIAM MCKINLEY
Arthur Mann—LA GUARDIA, VOL. I
Garrett Mattingly—THE ARMADA
John C. Miller—ALEXANDER HAMILTON
Samuel Eliot Morison—JOHN PAUL JONES
Carl Mydans—MORE THAN MEETS THE EYE
Allan Nevins—THE WAR FOR THE UNION, VOL. I
Charles Ogburn, Jr.—THE MARAUDERS
Vance Packard—THE STATUS SEEKERS
Berton Roueché—THE DELECTABLE MOUNTAINS
Arthur M. Schlesinger, Jr.—THE COMING OF THE NEW DEAL, VOL. II, THE
    AGE OF ROOSEVELT
George R. Stewart—PICKETT'S CHARGE
Elizabeth Thomas—THE HARMLESS PEOPLE
James Thurber—THE YEARS WITH ROSS

Poetry
(Nominees not Announced)

*Robert Lowell—LIFE STUDIES

1961

Fiction

*Conrad Richter—THE WATERS OF KRONOS
Louis Auchincloss—THE HOUSE OF FIVE TALENTS
Kay Boyle—GENERATION WITHOUT FAREWELL
John Hersey—THE CHILD BUYER
John Knowles—A SEPARATE PEACE
Harper Lee—TO KILL A MOCKINGBIRD
Wright Morris—CEREMONY IN A LONE TREE
Flannery O'Connor—THE VIOLENT BEAR IT AWAY
Elizabeth Spencer—THE LIGHT IN THE PIAZZA
Francis Steegmuller—THE CHRISTENING PARTY
John Updike—RABBIT, RUN
Mildred Walker—THE BODY OF A YOUNG MAN

Nonfiction

*William L. Shirer—THE RISE AND FALL OF THE THIRD REICH
Isaac Asimov—THE INTELLIGENT MAN'S GUIDE TO SCIENCE
Peter Blake—THE MASTER BUILDERS
George Dangerfield—CHANCELLOR ROBERT R. LIVINGSTON
David Donald—CHARLES SUMNER AND THE COMING OF THE CIVIL WAR
William O. Douglas—MY WILDERNESS
Loren Eiseley—FIRMAMENT OF TIME
John Graves—GOODBYE TO A RIVER
T. S. Mathews—NAME AND ADDRESS
Elizabeth Nowell—THOMAS WOLFE
Harlan B. Phillips—FELIX FRANKFURTER REMINISCES
Arthur M. Schlesinger, Jr.—THE POLITICS OF UPHEAVAL

Poetry

*Randall Jarrell—THE WOMAN AT THE WASHINGTON ZOO
W. H. Auden—HOMAGE TO CLIO
J. V. Cunningham—THE EXCLUSIONS OF RHYME
Robert Duncan—THE OPENING OF THE FIELD
Richard Eberhart—COLLECTED POEMS
Donald Justice—THE SUMMER ANNIVERSARIES
Howard Nemerov—NEW AND SELECTED POEMS
John Frederick Nims—KNOWLEDGE OF THE EVENING
Anne Sexton—TO BEDLAM AND PART WAY BACK
George Starbuck—BONE THOUGHTS
Eleanor Ross Taylor—WILDERNESS OF LADIES
Theodore Weiss—OUTLANDERS
Yvor Winters—COLLECTED POEMS

Fiction

*Walker Percy—THE MOVIEGOER
  Hortense Calisher—FALSE ENTRY
  George P. Elliott—AMONG THE DANGS
  Joseph Heller—CATCH-22
  Bernard Malamud—A NEW LIFE
  William Maxwell—THE CHATEAU
  J. D. Salinger—FRANNY AND ZOOEY
  Isaac Bashevis Singer—THE SPINOZA OF MARKET STREET
  Edward Lewis Wallant—THE PAWNBROKER
  Joan Williams—THE MORNING AND THE EVENING
  Richard Yates—REVOLUTIONARY ROAD

Nonfiction

*Lewis Mumford—THE CITY IN HISTORY: ITS ORIGINS, ITS TRANSFORMATIONS
  AND ITS PROSPECTS
  Robert Ardrey—AFRICAN GENESIS
  James Baldwin—NOBODY KNOWS MY NAME
  Stringfellow Barr—THE WILL OF ZEUS
  John Burchard and Albert Bush-Brown—THE ARCHITECTURE OF AMERICA
  René Dubos—THE DREAMS OF REASON
  Jane Jacobs—THE DEATH AND LIFE OF GREAT AMERICAN CITIES
  Oscar Lewis—THE CHILDREN OF SANCHEZ
  Virginia Peterson—A MATTER OF LIFE AND DEATH
  Mark Schorer—SINCLAIR LEWIS
  Elizabeth Stevenson—LAFCADIO HEARN
  Theodore H. White—THE MAKING OF THE PRESIDENT
  Ola Elizabeth Winslow—JOHN BUNYAN

Poetry

*Alan Dugan—POEMS
  Robert Bagg—MADONNA OF THE CELLO
  Philip Booth—THE ISLANDERS
  John Ciardi—IN THE STONEWORKS
  H. D. (Hilda Doolittle)—HELEN IN EGYPT
  Abbie Huston Evans—FACTS OF CRYSTAL
  Isabella Gardner—THE LOOKING GLASS
  Horace Gregory—MEDUSA IN GRAMERCY PARK
  John Holmes—THE FORTUNE TELLER
  Denise Levertov—JACOB'S LADDER
  Ned O'Gorman—ADAM BEFORE HIS MIRROR
  John Hall Wheelock—THE GARDENER AND OTHER POEMS

Fiction

*J. F. Powers—MORTE D'URBAN
    Vladimir Nabokov—PALE FIRE
    Katherine Anne Porter—SHIP OF FOOLS
    Dawn Powell—THE GOLDEN SPUR
    Clancy Sigal—GOING AWAY
    John Updike—PIGEON FEATHERS

Nonfiction

*Leon Edel—HENRY JAMES, VOL. II: THE CONQUEST OF LONDON; HENRY JAMES,
    VOL. III: THE MIDDLE YEARS
    Rachel Carson—SILENT SPRING
    Arthur and Barbara Gelb—O'NEILL
    Alfred Kazin—CONTEMPORARIES
    Frederic Morton—THE ROTHSCHILDS
    Ernest J. Simmons—CHEKHOV
    Page Smith—JOHN ADAMS
    Barbara W. Tuchman—THE GUNS OF AUGUST
    Edmund Wilson—PATRIOTIC GORE

Poetry

*William Stafford—TRAVELING THROUGH THE DARK
    Robert Creeley—FOR LOVE
    Donald F. Drummond—THE DRAWBRIDGE
    Robert Frost—IN THE CLEARING
    Kenneth Koch—THANK YOU AND OTHER POEMS
    Howard Nemerov—THE NEXT ROOM OF THE DREAM
    Winfield T. Scott—COLLECTED POEMS
    Anne Sexton—ALL MY PRETTY ONES
    William Carlos Williams—PICTURES FROM BRUEGHEL

Fiction

*John Updike—THE CENTAUR
    Bernard Malamud—IDIOTS FIRST
    Mary McCarthy—THE GROUP
    Thomas Pynchon—V
    Harvey Swados—THE WILL

Arts and Letters
(Nonfiction)

*Aileen Ward—JOHN KEATS: THE MAKING OF A POET

History and Biography
(Nonfiction)

*William H. McNeill—THE RISE OF THE WEST: A HISTORY OF THE HUMAN COMMUNITY

Science, Philosophy and Religion
(Nonfiction)

*Christopher Tunnard & Boris Pushkarev—MAN-MADE AMERICA

Nonfiction
(Leading Contenders for Above Subcategories)

James Baldwin—THE FIRE NEXT TIME
Walter Jackson Bate—JOHN KEATS
R. F. Dasmann—THE LAST HORIZON
Howard Ensign Evans—WASP FARM
Shelby Foote—THE CIVIL WAR, VOL. II
Nathan Glazer & Daniel P. Moynihan—BEYOND THE MELTING POT
Richard Hofstadter—ANTI-INTELLECTUALISM IN AMERICAN LIFE
David E. Lilienthal—CHANGE, HOPE AND THE BOMB
Seymour M. Lipset—THE FIRST NEW NATION
Peter Lyons—SUCCESS STORY: THE LIFE AND TIMES OF S. S. MCCLURE
Ralph McGill—THE SOUTH AND THE SOUTHERNER
Francis Steegmuller—APOLLINAIRE
Stewart Udall—THE QUIET CRISIS
Bertram D. Wolfe—THE FABULOUS LIFE OF DIEGO RIVERA

Poetry

*John Crowe Ransom—SELECTED POEMS
W. S. Merwin—THE MOVING TARGET
Louis Simpson—AT THE END OF THE OPEN ROAD
May Swenson—TO MIX WITH TIME

1965

Arts and Letters

*Eleanor Clark—OYSTERS OF LOCMARIAQUER
Eric Bentley—LIFE OF THE DRAMA
Robert Brustein—THE THEATER OF REVOLT

Edward Dahlberg—BECAUSE I WAS FLESH
Ralph Ellison—SHADOW AND ACT
Howard Mumford Jones—O STRANGE NEW WORLD: AMERICAN CULTURE,
THE FORMATIVE YEARS

Fiction

*Saul Bellow—HERZOG
Louis Auchincloss—THE RECTOR OF JUSTIN
John Hawkes—SECOND SKIN
Richard Kim—THE MARTYRED
Wallace Markfield—TO AN EARLY GRAVE
Vladimir Nabokov—THE DEFENSE
Isaac Bashevis Singer—SHORT FRIDAY

History and Biography

*Louis Fischer—THE LIFE OF LENIN
Oscar Lewis—PEDRO MARTINEZ: A MEXICAN PEASANT AND HIS FAMILY
R. R. Palmer—THE AGE OF DEMOCRATIC REVOLUTION
Willie Lee Rose—REHEARSAL FOR RECONSTRUCTION: THE PORT ROYAL
EXPERIMENT
Ernest Samuels—HENRY ADAMS: THE MAJOR PHASE
Richard J. Whelan—THE FOUNDING FATHER: THE STORY OF JOSEPH P.
KENNEDY

Poetry

*Theodore Roethke—THE FAR FIELD
Ben Belitt—THE ENEMY JOY
John Berryman—77 DREAM SONGS
James Dickey—HELMETS
Jean Garrigue—COUNTRY WITHOUT MAPS
Galway Kinnell—FLOWER HERDING ON MOUNT MONADNOCK
Robert Lowell—FOR THE UNION DEAD
William Meredith—THE WRECK OF THE THRESHER

Science, Philosophy and Religion

*Norbert Wiener—GOD AND GOLEM, INC.: A COMMENT ON CERTAIN POINTS
WHERE CYBERNETICS IMPINGES ON RELIGION
Walter Ciszek, S. J.—WITH GOD IN RUSSIA
Theodosius Dobzhansky—HEREDITY AND THE NATURE OF MAN
David Hawkins—THE LANGUAGE OF NATURE
John Courtney Murray, S. J.—THE PROBLEM OF GOD
Walter Sullivan—WE ARE NOT ALONE

Arts and Letters

*Janet Flanner—PARIS JOURNAL, 1944–65
 Alfred Kazin—STARTING OUT IN THE THIRTIES
 R. W. B. Lewis—TRIALS OF THE WORK
 Philip Rahv—THE MYTH AND THE POWERHOUSE
 Lionel Trilling—BEYOND CULTURE
 Rene Wellek—HISTORY OF MODERN CRITICISM

Fiction

*Katherine Anne Porter—THE COLLECTED STORIES OF KATHERINE ANNE PORTER
 Jesse Hill Ford—THE LIBERATION OF LORD BYRON JONES
 Peter Matthiessen—AT PLAY IN THE FIELDS OF THE LORD
 James Merrill—THE (DIBLOS) NOTEBOOK
 Flannery O'Connor—EVERYTHING THAT RISES MUST CONVERGE
 Harry Petrakis—PERICLES ON 31ST STREET

History and Biography

*Arthur M. Schlesinger, Jr.—A THOUSAND DAYS
 Irving Brant—THE BILL OF RIGHTS
 Edward Chase Kirkland—CHARLES FRANCIS ADAMS, JR.
 Richard B. Morris—THE PEACEMAKERS
 Robert Shaplen—THE LOST REVOLUTION
 Theodore H. White—THE MAKING OF THE PRESIDENT, 1964

Poetry

*James Dickey—BUCKDANCER'S CHOICE: POEMS
 W. H. Auden—ABOUT THE HOUSE
 Elizabeth Bishop—QUESTIONS OF TRAVEL
 Richard Eberhart—SELECTED POEMS
 Irving Feldman—THE PRIPET MARSHES
 Randall Jarrell—THE LOST WORLD
 Louis Simpson—SELECTED POEMS

Science, Philosophy and Religion
(no award given)

Charles Frankel—THE LOVE OF ANXIETY
Edgar Z. Friedenberg—COMING OF AGE IN AMERICA
Bentley Glass—SCIENCE AND ETHICAL VALUES
Alice Kimball Smith—A PERIL AND A HOPE

Arts and Letters

*Justin Kaplan—MR. CLEMENS AND MARK TWAIN: A BIOGRAPHY
Oliver Larkin—DAUMIER
Frederick A. Pottle—JAMES BOSWELL: THE EARLIER YEARS
Isaac Bashevis Singer—IN MY FATHER'S COURT
Susan Sontag—AGAINST INTERPRETATION
Lawrence Thompson—ROBERT FROST: THE EARLY YEARS

Fiction

*Bernard Malamud—THE FIXER
Louis Auchincloss—THE EMBEZZLER
Edwin O'Connor—ALL IN THE FAMILY
Walker Percy—THE LAST GENTLEMAN
Harry Petrakis—A DREAM OF KINGS
Wilfrid Sheed—OFFICE POLITICS

History and Biography

*Peter Gay—THE ENLIGHTENMENT: AN INTERPRETATION, VOL. I: THE RISE OF
MODERN PAGANISM
James H. Billington—THE ICON AND THE AXE
David Brion Davis—THE PROBLEM OF SLAVERY IN WESTERN CULTURE
Martin Duberman—JAMES RUSSELL LOWELL
Barrington Moore, Jr.—SOCIAL ORIGINS OF DICTATORSHIP AND DEMOCRACY
Peter Stansky & William Abrahams—JOURNEY TO THE FRONTIER

Poetry

*James Merrill—NIGHTS AND DAYS
John Ashbery—RIVERS AND MOUNTAINS
Barbara Howes—LOOKING UP AT LEAVES
Marianne Moore—TELL ME, TELL ME
Adrienne Rich—NECESSITIES OF LIFE
William Jay Smith—THE TIN CAN AND OTHER POEMS

Science, Philosophy and Religion

*Oscar Lewis—LA VIDA
Howard B. Adelman—MARCELLO MALPIGHI AND THE EVOLUTION OF
EMBRYOLOGY
George & Muriel Beadle—THE LANGUAGE OF LIFE
Wassily W. Leontief—ESSAYS IN ECONOMICS
Philip Rieff—THE TRIUMPH OF THE THERAPEUTIC
Erwin Straus—PHENOMENOLOGICAL PSYCHOLOGY

Translation

*Gregory Rabassa—JULIO CORTAZAR'S HOPSCOTCH
*Willard Trask—CASANOVA'S HISTORY OF MY LIFE
Ben Belitt—RAFAEL ALBERTI'S SELECTED POEMS
Ralph Manheim—CELINE'S DEATH ON THE INSTALLMENT PLAN

1968

Arts and Letters

*William Troy—SELECTED ESSAYS
R. P. Blackmur—A PRIMER OF IGNORANCE
Frank Conroy—STOP-TIME
Leonard B. Meyer—MUSIC, THE ARTS AND IDEAS
M. L. Rosenthal—THE NEW POETS
Stanley Weintraub—BEARDSLEY

Fiction

*Thornton Wilder—THE EIGHTH DAY
Norman Mailer—WHY ARE WE IN VIETNAM?
Joyce Carol Oates—A GARDEN OF EARTHLY DELIGHTS
Chaim Potok—THE CHOSEN
William Styron—THE CONFESSIONS OF NAT TURNER

History and Biography

*George F. Kennan—MEMOIRS: 1925–1950
H. W. Bragdon—WOODROW WILSON: THE ACADEMIC YEARS
Louis J. Halle—THE COLD WAR AS HISTORY
Roger Hilsman—TO MOVE A NATION
Nathan Silver—LOST NEW YORK

Poetry

*Robert Bly—THE LIGHT AROUND THE BODY
Denise Levertov—THE SORROW DANCE
W. S. Merwin—THE LICE
Kenneth Rexroth—COMPLETE POEMS
Louis Zukofsky—A-12

Science, Philosophy and Religion

*Jonathan Kozol—DEATH AT AN EARLY AGE
Theodosius Dobzhansky—THE BIOLOGY OF ULTIMATE CONCERN
John Kenneth Galbraith—THE NEW INDUSTRIAL STATE

Suzanne K. Langer—MIND: AN ESSAY ON HUMAN FEELING
Lewis Mumford—THE MYTH OF THE MACHINE

Translation

*Howard & Edna Hong—SØREN KIERKEGAARD'S JOURNALS & PAPERS
Elaine Gottlieb & Joseph Singer—ISAAC SINGER'S THE MANOR
Richmond Lattimore—THE ODYSSEY OF HOMER
Douglass Parker—ARISTOPHANES' THE CONGRESSWOMEN
Barbara Shelby—FREYRE'S MOTHER AND SON
L. B. Simpson—PRADO'S COUNTRY JUDGE
Arlene B. Werth—CHUKOVSKAYA'S THE DESERTED HOUSE

1969

Arts and Letters

*Norman Mailer—THE ARMIES OF THE NIGHT: HISTORY AS A NOVEL, THE NOVEL AS HISTORY
Hannah Arendt—MEN IN DARK TIMES
Peter Gay—WEIMAR CULTURE
Gordon S. Haight—GEORGE ELIOT
Gertrude Himmelfarb—VICTORIAN MINDS

Children's Literature

*Meindert DeJong—JOURNEY FROM PEPPERMINT STREET
Lloyd Alexander—THE HIGH KING
Patricia Clapp—CONSTANCE
Esther Hautzig—THE ENDLESS STEPPE
Milton Meltzer—LANGSTON HUGHES

Fiction

*Jerzy Kosinski—STEPS
John Barth—LOST IN THE FUNHOUSE
Frederick Exley—A FAN'S NOTES
Joyce Carol Oates—EXPENSIVE PEOPLE
Thomas Rogers—THE PURSUIT OF HAPPINESS

History and Biography

*Winthrop D. Jordan—WHITE OVER BLACK: AMERICAN ATTITUDES TOWARD THE NEGRO, 1550–1812
Noel Pharr Davis—LAWRENCE AND OPPENHEIMER
Alvin M. Josephy, Jr.—THE INDIAN HERITAGE OF AMERICA

Norman Mailer—MIAMI AND THE SIEGE OF CHICAGO: AN INFORMAL HISTORY
OF THE REPUBLICAN AND DEMOCRATIC CONVENTIONS OF 1968
David M. Potter—THE SOUTH AND THE SECTIONAL CONFLICT

Poetry

*John Berryman—HIS TOY, HIS DREAM, HIS REST
Gwendolyn Brooks—IN THE MECCA
Galway Kinnell—BODY RAGS
John Thompson—THE TALKING GIRL
Keith Waldrop—A WINDMILL NEAR CALVARY

The Sciences

*Robert J. Lifton—DEATH IN LIFE: SURVIVORS OF HIROSHIMA
René Dubos—SO HUMAN AN ANIMAL
Frank E. Manuel—A PORTRAIT OF ISAAC NEWTON
Karl Menninger, M.D.—THE CRIME OF PUNISHMENT
James D. Watson—THE DOUBLE HELIX

Translation

*William Weaver—CALVINO'S COSMICOMICS
Joseph Hitrec—ANDRIC'S THE PASHA'S CONCUBINE AND OTHER TALES
Rolfe Humphries—LUCRETIUS'S THE WAY THINGS ARE
Ellen Conroy Kennedy—CAMUS'S LYRICAL AND CRITICAL ESSAYS
Burton Watson—THE COMPLETE WORKS OF CHUANG TZU

––––––––––––––– 1970 –––––––––––––––

Arts and Letters

*Lillian Hellman—AN UNFINISHED WOMAN: A MEMOIR
Richard Howard—ALONE WITH AMERICA: ESSAYS ON THE ART OF POETRY IN
THE UNITED STATES SINCE 1950
Noel Perrin—DR. BOWDLER'S LEGACY: A HISTORY OF EXPURGATED BOOKS IN
ENGLAND AND AMERICA
John Unterecker—VOYAGE: A LIFE OF HART CRANE
Gore Vidal—REFLECTIONS UPON A SINKING SHIP

Children's Books

*Isaac Bashevis Singer—A DAY OF PLEASURE: STORIES OF A BOY GROWING UP IN
WARSAW
Vera and Bill Cleaver—WHERE THE LILIES BLOOM
Edna Mitchell Preston—POPCORN AND MA GOODNESS
William Steig—SYLVESTER AND THE MAGIC PEBBLE
Edwin Tunis—THE YOUNG UNITED STATES, 1783–1830

Fiction

*Joyce Carol Oates—THEM
    Leonard Gardner—FAT CITY
    Leonard Michaels—GOING PLACES
    Jean Stafford—THE COLLECTED STORIES OF JEAN STAFFORD
    Kurt Vonnegut, Jr.—SLAUGHTERHOUSE FIVE OR THE CHILDREN'S CRUSADE

History and Biography

*T. Harry Williams—HUEY LONG
    Dean Acheson—PRESENT AT THE CREATION: MY YEARS IN THE STATE
    DEPARTMENT
    Townsend Hoopes—THE LIMITS OF INTERVENTION
    John Womack, Jr.—ZAPATA AND THE MEXICAN REVOLUTION
    Gordon S. Wood—THE CREATION OF THE AMERICAN REPUBLIC

Philosophy and Religion

***Erik H. Erikson—GANDHI'S TRUTH: ON THE ORIGINS OF MILITANT
NONVIOLENCE**
    Kenneth E. Boulding—BEYOND ECONOMICS
    Loren Eiseley—THE UNEXPECTED UNIVERSE
    Rollo May—LOVE AND WILL
    Theodore Roszak—THE MAKING OF A COUNTER CULTURE

Poetry

*Elizabeth Bishop—THE COMPLETE POEMS
    Daniel Berrigan—FALSE GODS, REAL MEN
    Lawrence Ferlinghetti—THE SECRET MEANING OF THINGS
    Robert Lowell—NOTEBOOK, 1967–68
    Philip Whalen—ON BEAR'S HEAD

Translation

*Ralph Manheim—CELINE'S CASTLE TO CASTLE
    Denise Levertov—GUILLEVIC'S SELECTED POEMS
    Philippe Radley—BERBEROVA'S THE ITALICS ARE MINE
    Richard Seaver & Helen R. Lane—BRETON'S MANIFESTOS OF SURREALISM
    John Upton—SANCHEZ'S CUMBOTO

Arts and Letters

*Francis Steegmuller—COCTEAU: A BIOGRAPHY
Harold Bloom—YEATS
Robert Coles—ERIK H. ERIKSON
Nancy Milford—ZELDA
Lewis Mumford—THE MYTH OF THE MACHINE: THE PENTAGON OF POWER
Kenneth Rexroth—THE ALTERNATIVE SOCIETY

Children's Books

*Lloyd Alexander—THE MARVELOUS MISADVENTURES OF SEBASTIAN
Vera Cleaver & Bill Cleaver—GROVER
Paula Fox—BLOWFISH LIVE IN THE SEA
Arnold Lobel—FROG AND TOAD ARE FRIENDS
E. B. White—THE TRUMPET OF THE SWAN

Fiction

*Saul Bellow—MR. SAMMLER'S PLANET
James Dickey—DELIVERANCE
Shirley Hazzard—THE BAY OF NOON
John Updike—BECH: A BOOK
Eudora Welty—LOSING BATTLES

History and Biography

*James MacGregor Burns—ROOSEVELT: THE SOLDIER OF FREEDOM
David Donald—CHARLES SUMNER AND THE RIGHTS OF MAN
Andy Logan—AGAINST THE EVIDENCE: THE BECKER-ROSENTHAL AFFAIR
Dumas Malone—JEFFERSON THE PRESIDENT: FIRST TERM, 1801–1805
C. L. Sulzberger—THE LAST OF THE GIANTS

Poetry

*Mona Van Duyn—TO SEE, TO TAKE
Gregory Corso—ELEGIAC FEELINGS AMERICAN
W. S. Merwin—THE CARRIER OF LADDERS
Mark Strand—DARKER
May Swenson—ICONOGRAPHS

The Sciences

*Raymond Phineas Sterns—SCIENCE IN THE BRITISH COLONIES OF AMERICA
Gustav Eckstein—THE BODY HAS A HEAD
Victor C. Ferkiss—TECHNOLOGICAL MAN
Ian L. McHarg—DESIGN WITH NATURE
Theodore Rosebury—LIFE OF MAN

Translation

*Frank Jones—BRECHT'S SAINT JOAN OF THE STOCKYARDS
*Edward G. Seidensticker—YASUNARI KAWABATA'S THE SOUND OF THE MOUNTAIN
    Joseph Barnes—PLATONOV'S THE FIERCE AND BEAUTIFUL WORLD
    Richard Howard—JEAN COCTEAU'S AUTOBIOGRAPHY, PROFESSIONAL SECRETS
    Norman R. Shapiro—FEYDEAU'S FOUR FARCES

1972

Arts and Letters

*Charles Rosen—THE CLASSICAL STYLE: HAYDN, MOZART, BEETHOVEN
    M. H. Abrams—NATURAL SUPERNATURALISM: TRADITION AND REVOLUTION IN ROMANTIC LITERATURE
    James Dickey—SORTIES
    Thomas R. Edwards—IMAGINATION AND POWER: A STUDY OF POETRY ON PUBLIC THEMES
    Norman Fruman—COLERIDGE, THE DAMAGED ARCHANGEL
    Cesar Grana—FACT AND SYMBOL: ESSAYS IN THE SOCIOLOGY OF ART AND LITERATURE
    B. H. Haggin—BALLET CHRONICLE
    Nathan Irvin Huggins—HARLEM RENAISSANCE
    Iris Origo—IMAGES AND SHADOWS
    John Simon—MOVIES INTO FILMS: FILM CRITICISM, 1967–1970

Biography

*Joseph P. Lash—ELEANOR AND FRANKLIN: THE STORY OF THEIR RELATIONSHIP, BASED ON ELEANOR ROOSEVELT'S PRIVATE PAPERS
    John Cody—AFTER GREAT PAIN: THE INNER LIFE OF EMILY DICKINSON
    Emily Farnham—CHARLES DEMUTH
    David Freeman Hawke—BENJAMIN RUSH
    Ralph Ketcham—JAMES MADISON
    Harding Lemay—INSIDE, LOOKING OUT: A PERSONAL MEMOIR
    D'Arcy McNickle—INDIAN MAN: A LIFE OF OLIVER LA FARGE
    Ronald Paulson—HOGARTH, VOL. II
    Lacey Baldwin Smith—HENRY VIII
    Barbara W. Tuchman—STILLWELL AND THE AMERICAN EXPERIENCE IN CHINA, 1911–45

Children's Books

*Donald Barthelme—THE SLIGHTLY IRREGULAR FIRE ENGINE OR THE HITHERING THITHERING DJINN
    Jan Adkins—THE ART AND INDUSTRY OF SANDCASTLES
    John Donovan—WILD IN THE WORLD

Virginia Hamilton—THE PLANET OF JUNIOR BROWN
June Jordan—HIS OWN WHERE
Ursula K. Le Guin—THE TOMBS OF ATUAN
Robert C. O'Brien—MRS. FRISBY AND THE RATS OF NIMH
Chela Duran Ryan—HILDILID'S NIGHT
Marilyn Sachs—THE BEAR'S HOUSE
William Steig—AMOS & BORIS
Clyde Watson—FATHER FOX'S PENNYRHYMES

Contemporary Affairs

*Stewart Brand, ed.—THE LAST WHOLE EARTH CATALOG
Ronald J. Glasser—365 DAYS
Richard Hammer—THE COURT-MARTIAL OF LT. CALLEY
Larry L. King—CONFESSIONS OF A WHITE RACIST
Norman Mailer—THE PRISONER OF SEX
Victor S. Navasky—KENNEDY JUSTICE
Don Oberdorfer—TET!
Mike Royko—BOSS: RICHARD J. DALEY OF CHICAGO
William Irwin Thompson—AT THE EDGE OF HISTORY
Tom Wolfe—RADICAL CHIC: MAU-MAUING THE FLAK CATCHERS

Fiction

*Flannery O'Connor—THE COMPLETE STORIES OF FLANNERY O'CONNOR
Frederick Buechner—LION COUNTRY
E. L. Doctorow—THE BOOK OF DANIEL
Stanley Elkin—THE DICK GIBSON SHOW
Tom McHale—FARRAGAN'S RETREAT
Joyce Carol Oates—WONDERLAND
Cynthia Ozick—THE PAGAN RABBI AND OTHER STORIES
Walker Percy—LOVE AMONG THE RUINS
Earl Thompson—A GARDEN OF SAND
John Updike—RABBIT REDUX

History

*Allan Nevins—ORDEAL OF THE UNION, VOLS. VII & VIII: THE ORGANIZED WAR,
1863–1864, and THE ORGANIZED WAR TO VICTORY
John Malcolm Brinnin—THE SWAY OF THE GRAND SALOON: A SOCIAL
HISTORY OF THE NORTH ATLANTIC
Carl N. Degler—NEITHER BLACK NOR WHITE: SLAVERY AND RACE RELATIONS
IN BRAZIL AND THE UNITED STATES
Oscar & Mary F. Handlin—FACING LIFE: YOUTH AND THE FAMILY IN
AMERICAN HISTORY
Elizabeth Janeway—MAN'S WORLD, WOMAN'S PLACE: A STUDY IN SOCIAL
MYTHOLOGY
Howard Mumford Jones—THE AGE OF ENERGY: VARIETIES OF AMERICAN
EXPERIENCE, 1865–1915
Clarence G. Lasby—PROJECT PAPERCLIP: GERMAN SCIENTISTS AND THE COLD
WAR

Samuel Eliot Morison—THE EUROPEAN DISCOVERY OF AMERICA: THE NORTHERN VOYAGES, A. D. 500–1600
David J. Rothman—THE DISCOVERY OF THE ASYLUM: SOCIAL ORDER AND DISORDER IN THE NEW REPUBLIC
Raymond J. Sontag—A BROKEN WORLD, 1919–1939

Philosophy and Religion

*Martin E. Marty—RIGHTEOUS EMPIRE: THE PROTESTANT EXPERIENCE IN AMERICA
Robert N. Bellah—BEYOND BELIEF: ESSAYS ON RELIGION IN A POST-TRADITIONAL WORLD
Noam Chomsky—PROBLEMS OF KNOWLEDGE AND FREEDOM
Philip Garvin & Arthur A. Cohen—A PEOPLE APART: HASIDISM IN AMERICA
Joel Kovell—WHITE RACISM: A PSYCHOHISTORY
William G. McLoughlin—NEW ENGLAND DISSENT, 1630–1883, VOL. II: THE BAPTISTS AND THE SEPARATION OF CHURCH AND STATE
Jaroslav Pelikan—THE EMERGENCE OF THE CATHOLIC TRADITION, 100–600
John Rawls—A THEORY OF JUSTICE
Ernest R. Sandeen—ROOTS OF FUNDAMENTALISM: BRITISH AND AMERICAN MILLENARIANISM, 1800–1930
B. F. Skinner—BEYOND FREEDOM AND DIGNITY

Poetry

*Howard Moss—SELECTED POEMS
*Frank O'Hara—THE COLLECTED WORKS OF FRANK O'HARA
A. R. Ammons—BRIEFINGS: POEMS SMALL AND EASY
Jon Anderson—DEATH & FRIENDS
Robert Fitzgerald—SPRING SHADE: POEMS, 1931–1970
Robert Hayden—POEMS IN THE MOURNING TIME
John Hollander—THE NIGHT MIRROR
Galway Kinnell—THE BOOK OF NIGHTMARES
David Shapiro—MAN HOLDING AN ACOUSTIC PANEL
Allen Tate—THE SWIMMERS AND OTHER SELECTED POEMS
James Wright—COLLECTED POEMS

The Sciences

*George L. Small—THE BLUE WHALE
Elizabeth Barlow—THE FORESTS AND WETLANDS OF NEW YORK CITY
Barry Commoner—THE CLOSING CIRCLE: NATURE, MAN AND TECHNOLOGY
Nathan G. Hale, Jr.—FREUD AND THE AMERICANS: THE BEGINNINGS OF PSYCHOANALYSIS IN THE UNITED STATES, 1876–1917
Bruce C. Heezen & Charles D. Hollister—THE FACE OF THE DEEP
David Leveson—A SENSE OF THE EARTH
Norman Mailer—OF A FIRE ON THE MOON
John McPhee—ENCOUNTER WITH THE ARCHDRUID
Charles A. Whitney—THE DISCOVERY OF OUR GALAXY
Edward O. Wilson—THE INSECT SOCIETIES

Translation

*Austryn Wainhouse—JACQUES MONOD'S CHANCE AND NECESSITY
E. B. Ashton—KARL JASPERS'S PHILOSOPHY, VOL. III
Charles Boer—HOMER'S THE HOMERIC HYMNS
Albert Hofstadter—HEIDEGGER'S POETRY, LANGUAGE, THOUGHT
Ralph Manheim—YAMO OULOGUEM'S BOUND TO VIOLENCE
Herbert Mason—GILGAMESH
Raymond Rosenthal—LANDOLF'S CANCERQUEEN AND OTHER STORIES
Richard Sheldon—SHKLOVSKY'S ZOO OR LETTERS NOT ABOUT LOVE
Richard Wilbur—MOLIÈRE'S THE SCHOOL FOR WIVES
Richard & Clara Winston—LETTERS OF THOMAS MANN, 1889–1955

1973

Arts and Letters

*Arthur M. Wilson—DIDEROT
Leo Braudy—JEAN RENOIR: THE WORLD OF HIS FILMS
Arlene Croce—THE FRED ASTAIRE & GINGER ROGERS BOOK
Stanley E. Fish—SELF-CONSUMING ARTIFACTS: THE EXPERIENCE OF
SEVENTEENTH-CENTURY LITERATURE
Michael Goldman—SHAKESPEARE AND THE ENERGIES OF DRAMA
Paul Goodman—SPEAKING AND LANGUAGE: DEFENSE OF POETRY
Daniel Hoffman—POE POE POE POE POE POE POE
Albert Murray—SOUTH TO A VERY OLD PLACE
Linda Nochlin—REALISM
Harold Rosenberg—THE DE-DEFINITION OF ART: ACTION ART TO POP TO
EARTHWORKS
Leo Steinberg—OTHER CRITERIA: CONFRONTATIONS WITH TWENTIETH-
CENTURY ART
Lionel Trilling—SINCERITY AND AUTHENTICITY
Alec Wilder—AMERICAN POPULAR SONG: THE GREAT INNOVATORS,
1900–1950
Vernon Young—ON FILM: UNPOPULAR ESSAYS ON A POPULAR ART

Biography

*James Thomas Flexner—GEORGE WASHINGTON, VOL. IV: ANGUISH AND
FAREWELL, 1793–1799
Ingrid Bengis—COMBAT IN THE EROGENOUS ZONE
Hortense Calisher—HERSELF
Kenneth S. Davis—FDR: THE BECKONING OF DESTINY, 1882–1928
Leon Edel—HENRY JAMES, VOL. V: THE MASTER, 1901–1916
Eleanor Flexner—MARY WOLLSTONECRAFT
Nikki Giovanni—GEMINI

John Houseman—RUN-THROUGH
Diane Johnson—LESSER LIVES
George F. Kennan—MEMOIRS, 1950–1963
Joseph P. Lash—ELEANOR: THE YEARS ALONE
Margaret Mead—BLACKBERRY WINTER: MY EARLIER YEARS
Peter Stansky & William Abrahams—THE UNKNOWN ORWELL

Children's Books

*Ursula K. Le Guin—THE FARTHEST SHORE
Betsy Byars—THE HOUSE OF WINGS
Ingri & Edgar Parin d'Aulaire—TROLLS
Jean Craighead George—JULIE OF THE WOLVES
Betty Jean Lifton & Thomas C. Fox—CHILDREN OF VIETNAM
Georgess McHargue—THE IMPOSSIBLE PEOPLE
Zilpha Keatley Snyder—THE WITCHES OF WORM
William Steig—DOMINIC

Contemporary Affairs

*Frances FitzGerald—FIRE IN THE LAKE: THE VIETNAMESE AND THE AMERICANS IN VIETNAM
Michael Barone, Grant Ujifusa & Douglas Mathews—THE ALMANAC OF AMERICAN POLITICS
Herbert Block—HERBLOCK'S STATE OF THE UNION
Lynn Eden—CRISIS IN WATERTOWN
David Halberstam—THE BEST AND THE BRIGHTEST
Seymour Hersh—COVER-UP
Stanley Karnow—MAO AND CHINA
Richard Sennett & Jonathan Cobb—THE HIDDEN INJURIES OF CLASS
Colin M. Turnbull—THE MOUNTAIN PEOPLE
Garry Wills—BARE RUINED CHOIRS
(no specific author)—ATTICA: THE OFFICIAL REPORT OF THE NEW YORK STATE SPECIAL COMMISSION ON ATTICA

Fiction

*John Barth—CHIMERA
*John Williams—AUGUSTUS
Brock Brower—THE LATE GREAT CREATURE
Alan Friedman—HERMAPHRODEITY
Barry Hannah—GERONIMO REX
George V. Higgins—THE FRIENDS OF EDDIE COYLE
R. M. Koster—THE PRINCE
Vladimir Nabokov—TRANSPARENT THINGS
Ishmael Reed—MUMBO JUMBO
Thomas Rogers—THE CONFESSIONS OF A CHILD OF THE CENTURY
Isaac Bashevis Singer—ENEMIES, A LOVE STORY
Eudora Welty—THE OPTIMIST'S DAUGHTER

History

*Robert Manson Myers—THE CHILDREN OF PRIDE
*Isaiah Trunk—JUDENRAT
    James D. Barber—PRESIDENTIAL CHARACTER
    John P. Diggins—MUSSOLINI AND FASCISM
    Richard Dunn—SUGAR AND SLAVES
    Loren B. Graham—SCIENCE AND PHILOSOPHY IN THE SOVIET UNION
    David Lovejoy—GLORIOUS REVOLUTION IN AMERICA
    Jerre Mangione—THE DREAM AND THE DEAL
    Robert O. Paxton—VICHY FRANCE
    Edward R. Rice—MAO'S WAY

Philosophy and Religion

*S. E. Ahlstrom—A RELIGIOUS HISTORY OF THE AMERICAN PEOPLE
    Silvano Arieti—THE WILL TO BE HUMAN
    Germaine Bree—CAMUS AND SARTRE
    Stanley Cavell—THE SENSES OF WALDEN
    William A. Christian, Jr.—PERSON AND GOD IN A SPANISH VALLEY
    Arthur C. Danto—MYSTICISM AND MORALITY
    William Leiss—THE DOMINATION OF NATURE
    Theodore Roszak—WHERE THE WASTELAND ENDS
    Morton White—SCIENCE AND SENTIMENT IN AMERICA
    Theodore Ziolkowski—FICTIONAL TRANSFIGURATION OF JESUS

Poetry

*A. R. Ammons—COLLECTED POEMS, 1951–1971
    W. H. Auden—EPISTLE TO A GODSON AND OTHER POEMS
    John Berryman—DELUSIONS, ETC.
    Richard Eberhart—FIELDS OF GRACE
    Samuel Hazo—ONCE FOR THE LAST BANDIT
    John Hollander—TOWN AND COUNTRY MATTERS
    Denise Levertov—FOOTPRINTS
    Archibald MacLeish—THE HUMAN SEASON
    James Merrill—BRAVING THE ELEMENTS
    Frederick Morgan—A BOOK OF CHANGE
    Ishmael Reed—CONJURE
    Louis Simpson—ADVENTURES OF THE LETTER I

The Sciences

*George B. Schaller—THE SERENGETI LION: A STUDY OF PREDATOR-PREY
RELATIONS
    John E. Bardach, John H. Ryther & William O. McLarney—AQUACULTURE
    Herman H. Goldstine—THE COMPUTER FROM PASCAL TO VON NEUMANN
    Garrett Hardin—EXPLORING NEW ETHICS FOR SURVIVAL
    Morris Kline—MATHEMATICAL THOUGHT FROM ANCIENT TO MODERN TIMES
    Peter Matthiessen & Eliot Porter—THE TREE WHERE MAN WAS BORN/THE
AFRICAN EXPERIENCE

H. Lewis McKinney—WALLACE AND NATURAL SELECTION
Victor Richards, M. D.—CANCER
Ann H. Zwinger & Beatrice E. Willard—LAND ABOVE THE TREES

Translation

*Allen Mandelbaum—THE AENEID OF VIRGIL
Lily Feiler—SHKLOVSKY'S MAYAKOVSKY AND HIS CIRCLE
Michael Gallagher—YUKIO MISHIMA'S SPRING SNOW
Richard Howard—CAMUS'S A HAPPY DEATH
Edmund Keeley & Phillip Sherrard—CAVAFY'S SELECTED POEMS
Isaac Kelin—THE BOOK OF WOMEN
Eleanor L. M. Schmidt—VON HAXTHAUSEN'S STUDIES ON THE INTERIOR OF RUSSIA
May Swenson—TRANSTROMER'S WINDOWS AND STONES
Victor Terras—DOSTOEVSKY'S THE GAMBLER

1974

Arts and Letters

*Pauline Kael—DEEPER INTO THE MOVIES
Daniel Aaron—THE UNWRITTEN WAR
W. H. Auden—FOREWORDS AND AFTERWORDS
Clarence Brown—MANDELSTAM
Richard Ellmann—GOLDEN CODGERS
B. H. Haggin—A DECADE OF MUSIC
Lillian Hellman—PENTIMENTO
Edward Hoagland—WALKING THE DEAD DIAMOND RIVER
Lincoln Kirstein—ELIE NADELMAN
Leonard B. Meyer—EXPLAINING MUSIC
Kevin Starr—AMERICANS AND THE CALIFORNIA DREAM
Saul Steinberg—THE INSPECTOR

Biography

*John Clive—MACAULAY: THE SHAPING OF THE HISTORIAN (ALSO WON HISTORY AWARD)
*Douglas Day—MALCOLM LOWRY: A BIOGRAPHY
J. H. Adamson & H. F. Folland—SIR HARRY VANE
Robert V. Bruce—BELL
Stephen F. Cohen—BUKHARIN AND THE BOLSHEVIK REVOLUTION
Lester G. Crocker—JEAN-JACQUES ROUSSEAU: THE PROPHETIC VOICE, VOL. II
Myra Friedman—BURIED ALIVE
William H. Harbaugh—LAWYER'S LAWYER
Townsend Hoopes—THE DEVIL AND JOHN FOSTER DULLES
Louis Sheaffer—O'NEILL

Kathryn Kish Sklar—CATHERINE BEECHER
Adam B. Ulam—STALIN

Children's Books

*Eleanor Cameron—THE COURT OF THE STONE CHILDREN
Alice Childress—A HERO AIN'T NOTHIN' BUT A SANDWICH
Vera and Bill Cleaver—THE WHYS AND WHEREFORES OF LITTABELLE LEE
Julia Cunningham—THE TREASURE IS THE ROSE
Bette Greene—SUMMER OF MY GERMAN SOLDIER
Kristin Hunter—GUESTS IN THE PROMISED LAND
E. L. Konigsburg—A PROUD TASTE FOR SCARLET AND MINIVER
Norma Fox Mazer—A FIGURE OF SPEECH
F. N. Monjo—POOR RICHARD IN FRANCE
Harve Zemach—DUFFY AND THE DEVIL

Contemporary Affairs

*Murray Kempton—THE BRIAR PATCH
Peter Davies—THE TRUTH ABOUT KENT STATE
John Kenneth Galbraith—ECONOMICS
Vivian Gornick—IN SEARCH OF ALI MAHMOUD
Walter Karp—INDISPENSABLE ENEMIES
Robert J. Lifton—HOME FROM THE WAR
Jessica Mitford—KIND AND USUAL PUNISHMENT
Nora Sayre—SIXTIES GOING ON SEVENTIES
Arthur M. Schlesinger, Jr.—THE IMPERIAL PRESIDENCY
Robert Sherill—THE SATURDAY NIGHT SPECIAL AND OTHER GUNS

Fiction

*Thomas Pynchon—GRAVITY'S RAINBOW
*Isaac Bashevis Singer—A CROWN OF FEATHERS AND OTHER STORIES
Doris Betts—BEASTS OF THE WORLD AND OTHER STORIES
John Cheever—THE WORLD OF APPLES
Ellen Douglas—APOSTLES OF LIGHT
Stanley Elkin—SEARCHES AND SEIZURES
John Gardner—NICKEL MOUNTAIN
John Leonard—BLACK CONCEIT
Thomas McGuane—NINETY-TWO IN THE SHADE
Wilfrid Sheed—PEOPLE WILL ALWAYS BE KIND
Gore Vidal—BURR
Joy Williams—STATE OF GRACE

History

*John Clive—MACAULAY: THE SHAPING OF THE HISTORIAN (ALSO WON BIOGRAPHY
AWARD)
Ray Allen Billington—FREDERICK JACKSON TURNER
Daniel J. Boorstin—THE AMERICANS: THE DEMOCRATIC EXPERIENCE
Frank Freidel—FRANKLIN D. ROOSEVELT

Lawrence M. Friedman—A HISTORY OF AMERICAN LAW
Frederic C. Lane—VENICE
Edward Pessen—RICHES, CLASS AND POWER BEFORE THE CIVIL WAR
Richard Slotkin—REGENERATION THROUGH VIOLENCE
Stephen Thernstrom—THE OTHER BOSTONIANS
Robert C. Tucker—STALIN AS REVOLUTIONARY

Philosophy and Religion

*Maurice Natanson—EDMUND HUSSERL: PHILOSOPHER OF INFINITE TASKS
Don S. Browning—GENERATIVE MAN
Harvey Cox—THE SEDUCTION OF THE SPIRIT
Erich Fromm—THE ANATOMY OF HUMAN DESTRUCTIVENESS
Marjorie Grene—SARTRE
Trent Schroyer—THE CRITIQUE OF DOMINATION
Laurence Veysey—THE COMMUNAL EXPERIENCE
Frederick Wakeman, Jr.—HISTORY AND WILL
Harry Austryn Wolfson—STUDIES IN THE HISTORY OF PHILOSOPHY AND
   RELIGION
Larzer Ziff—PURITANISM IN AMERICA

Poetry

*Allen Ginsberg—THE FALL OF AMERICA: POEMS OF THESE STATES, 1965-1971.
*Adrienne Rich—DIVING INTO THE WRECK: POEMS 1971–1972
Hayden Carruth—FROM SNOW AND ROCK, FROM CHAOS
Evan S. Connell, Jr.—POINTS FOR A COMPASS ROSE
Peter Everwine—COLLECTING THE ANIMALS
Richard Hugo—THE LADY IN KICKING HORSE RESERVOIR
Donald Justice—DEPARTURES
Eleanor Lerman—ARMED LOVE
Audre Lorde—FROM A LAND WHERE OTHER PEOPLE LIVE
Alice Walker—REVOLUTIONARY PETUNIAS AND OTHER POEMS
Charles Wright—HARD FREIGHT

The Sciences

*S. E. Luria—LIFE: THE UNFINISHED EXPERIMENT
Jeremy Bernstein—EINSTEIN
Theodosius Dobzhansky—GENETIC DIVERSITY & HUMAN EQUALITY
Amitai Etzioni—GENETIC FIX
J. M. Jauch—ARE QUANTA REAL?
Ruth Kirk—DESERT
Suzanne K. Langer—MIND, VOL. II
George Laycock—AUTUMN OF THE EAGLE
Robert I. Levy—TAHITIANS
William T. Powers—BEHAVIOR
Edwin S. Schneidman—DEATHS OF MAN

Translation

*Karen Brazell—THE CONFESSIONS OF LADY NIJO
*Helen R. Lane—OCTAVIO PAZ'S ALTERNATING CURRENT
*Jackson Matthews—PAUL VALERY'S MONSIEUR TESTE
    Kimon Friar—MODERN GREEK POETRY
    Anthony Hecht & Helen H. Bacon—AESCHYLUS'S SEVEN AGAINST THEBES
    Anthony Kerrigan—MIGUEL D. UNAMUNO'S THE TRAGIC SENSE OF LIFE IN MEN AND NATIONS
    Michael Kowal—CURTIUS'S ESSAYS ON EUROPEAN LITERATURE
    Ralph Manheim—GUNTER GRASS'S FROM THE DIARY OF A SNAIL
    W. S. Merwin—ASIAN FIGURES
    Burton Watson—THE OLD MAN WHO DOES AS HE PLEASES: SELECTIONS FROM THE POETRY AND PROSE OF LU YU
    Sophie Wilkins—THOMAS BERNHARD'S THE LIME WORKS

1975

Arts and Letters

*Roger Shattuck—MARCEL PROUST
*Lewis Thomas—THE LIVES OF A CELL: NOTES OF A BIOLOGY WATCHER (also won Sciences award)
    Calvin Bedient—EIGHT CONTEMPORARY POETS
    Alessandra Comini—EGON SCHIELE'S PORTRAITS
    Peter Gay—STYLE IN HISTORY
    Richard Gilman—THE MAKING OF MODERN DRAMA
    Elizabeth Hardwick—SEDUCTION AND BETRAYAL
    Marjorie L. Hoover—MEYERHOLD
    H. W. Janson—SIX STUDIES
    Eleanor Perenyi—LISZT
    Oliver Strunk—ESSAYS ON MUSIC IN THE MODERN WORLD

Biography

*Richard B. Sewall—THE LIFE OF EMILY DICKINSON
    Richard R. Beeman—PATRICK HENRY
    Michael Collins—CARRYING THE FIRE
    Ben Maddow—EDWARD WESTON
    James R. Mellow—CHARMED CIRCLE
    Francis Steegmuller—"YOUR ISADORA"
    Wallace Stegner—THE UNEASY CHAIR: A BIOGRAPHY OF BERNARD DE VOTO
    Richard M. Sudhalter & Philip R. Evans—BIX
    Glenn Watkins—GESUALDO
    James A. Weisheipl—FRIAR THOMAS D'AQUINO

Children's Books

*Virginia Hamilton—M. C. HIGGINS THE GREAT
Natalie Babbitt—THE DEVIL'S STORYBOOK
Bruce Buchenholz—DOCTOR IN THE ZOO
Bruce Clements—I TELL A LIE EVERY SO OFTEN
James Lincoln Collier & Christopher Collier—MY BROTHER SAM IS DEAD
Jason Laure & Ettagale Laure—JOI BANGLA! THE CHILDREN OF BANGLADESH
Milton Meltzer—REMEMBER THE DAYS
Milton Meltzer—WORLD OF OUR FATHERS
Adrienne Richard—WINGS
Mary Stolz—THE EDGE OF NEXT YEAR

Contemporary Affairs

*Theodore Rosengarten—ALL GOD'S DANGERS: THE LIFE OF NATE SHAW
Raoul Berger—EXECUTIVE PRIVILEGE
Carl Bernstein & Bob Woodward—ALL THE PRESIDENT'S MEN
Robert Campbell—THE CHASM
Robert A. Caro—THE POWER BROKER
Joe Eszterhas—CHARLIE SIMPSON'S APOCALYPSE
Middleton Harris, Ed.—THE BLACK BOOK
Andrew Levinson—THE WORKING CLASS MAJORITY
Robert M. Pirsig—ZEN AND THE ART OF MOTORCYCLE MAINTENANCE
Franz Schurman—THE LOGIC OF WORLD POWER
Rachel Scott—MUSCLE AND BLOOD
Studs Terkel—WORKING

Fiction

*Robert Stone—DOG SOLDIERS
*Thomas Williams—THE HAIR OF HAROLD ROUX
Donald Barthelme—GUILTY PLEASURES
Gail Godwin—THE ODD WOMAN
Joseph Heller—SOMETHING HAPPENED
Toni Morrison—SULA
Vladimir Nabokov—LOOK AT THE HARLEQUINS!
Grace Paley—ENORMOUS CHANGES AT THE LAST MINUTE
Philip Roth—MY LIFE AS A MAN
Mark Smith—THE DEATH OF A DETECTIVE

History

*Bernard Bailyn—THE ORDEAL OF THOMAS HUTCHINSON
Paul Boyer & Stephen Nissenbaum—SALEM POSSESSED
Robert Brentano—ROME BEFORE AVIGNON
Shelby Foote—THE CIVIL WAR
Eugene D. Genovese—ROLL, JORDAN, ROLL
John R. Gillis—YOUTH AND HISTORY
Erich S. Gruen—THE LAST GENERATION OF THE ROMAN REPUBLIC

Christopher H. Johnson—UTOPIAN COMMUNISM IN FRANCE
Gerald H. Meaker—THE REVOLUTIONARY LEFT IN SPAIN
Edward Shorter & Charles Tilly—STRIKES IN FRANCE
Mira Wilkins—THE MATURING OF MULTINATIONAL ENTERPRISE
Peter H. Wood—BLACK MAJORITY

Philosophy and Religion

*Robert Nozick—ANARCHY, STATE AND UTOPIA
Ian G. Barbour—MYTHS, MODELS AND PARADIGMS
Leonard E. Barrett—SOUL-FORCE
John Murray Cuddihy—THE ORDEAL OF CIVILITY
Philip Garvin & Julia Welch—RELIGIOUS AMERICA
Guenter Lewy—RELIGION AND REVOLUTION
Barbara G. Meyerhoff—PEYOTE HUNT
Jaroslav Pelikan—THE SPIRIT OF EASTERN CHRISTENDOM, VOL. II
Rosemary Radford Ruether—FAITH AND FRATRICIDE

Poetry

*Marilyn Hacker—PRESENTATION PIECE
A. R. Ammons—SPHERE
John Balaban—AFTER OUR WAR
Albert Goldbarth—JAN. 31
Richard Howard—TWO-PART INVENTIONS
Josephine Jacobsen—THE SHADE-SELLER
Michael Ryan—THREATS INSTEAD OF TREES
Susan Fromberg Schaeffer—GRANITE LADY
David Wagoner—SLEEPING IN THE WOODS
Reed Whittemore—THE MOTHER'S BREAST AND THE FATHER'S HOUSE

The Sciences

*Silvano Arieti—INTERPRETATION OF SCHIZOPHRENIA
*Lewis Thomas—THE LIVES OF A CELL: NOTES OF A BIOLOGY WATCHER (also won Arts and Letters award)
Lewis S. Feuer—EINSTEIN AND THE GENERATION OF SCIENCE
Howard E. Gruber & Paul Barrett—DARWIN ON MAN
J. L. Heilbron—H. G. J. MOSELEY
Richard S. Lewis—THE VOYAGES OF APOLLO
John McPhee—THE CURVE OF BINDING ENERGY
Stanley Milgram—OBEDIENCE TO AUTHORITY
Walter Sullivan—CONTINENTS IN MOTION
Dorothy B. Vitaliano—LEGENDS OF THE EARTH

Translation

*Anthony Kerrigan—MIGUEL D. UNAMUNO'S THE AGONY OF CHRISTIANITY AND ESSAYS ON FAITH
Clarence Brown & W. S. Merwin—MANDELSTAM'S SELECTED POEMS
Sheila Cudahy—NATALIA GINZBURG'S NO WAY
Norman Thomas di Giovanni—BORGES'S IN PRAISE OF DARKNESS

Michael Kandel—STANISLAW LEM'S THE CYBERIAD and THE FUTUROLOGICAL CONGRESS
Peter Kussi—KUNDERA'S LIFE IS ELSEWHERE
Helen R. Lane—CLAUDE SIMON'S CONDUCTING BODIES
Ralph Manheim—HERMANN BROCH'S THE GUILTLESS
Raymond Rosenthal—PIETRO CITATI'S GOETHE
William Weaver—ITALIO CALVINO'S INVISIBLE CITIES

1976

Arts and Letters

*Paul Fussell—THE GREAT WAR AND MODERN MEMORY
Lincoln Kirstein—NIJINSKY DANCING
Lawrence L. Langer—THE HOLOCAUST AND THE LITERARY IMAGINATION
Robert Rosenblum—MODERN PAINTING AND THE NORTHERN ROMANTIC TRADITION
Patricia Meyer Spacks—THE FEMALE IMAGINATION
Leo Steinberg—MICHELANGELO'S LAST PAINTINGS

Children's Literature

*Walter D. Edmonds—BERT BREEN'S BARN
Eleanor Cameron—TO THE GREEN MOUNTAINS
Norma Faber—AS I WAS CROSSING BOSTON COMMON
Isabelle Holland—OF LOVE AND DEATH AND OTHER JOURNEYS
David McCord—THE STAR IN THE PAIL
Nicholasa Mohr—EL BRONX REMEMBERED
Brenda Wilkinson—LUDELL

Contemporary Affairs

*Michael J. Arlen—PASSAGE TO ARARAT
Richard J. Barnet & Ronald E. Muller—GLOBAL REACH
Peter L. Berger—PYRAMIDS OF SACRIFICE
John Kenneth Galbraith—MONEY
Eugene W. Smith & Aileen M. Smith—MINAMATA
Tim Wicker—A TIME TO DIE

Fiction

*William Gaddis—JR
Saul Bellow—HUMBOLDT'S GIFT
Hortense Calisher—THE COLLECTED STORIES OF HORTENSE CALISHER
Johanna Kaplan—OTHER PEOPLE'S LIVES
Vladimir Nabokov—TYRANTS DESTROYED AND OTHER STORIES
Larry Woiwode—BEYOND THE BEDROOM WALL

History and Biography

*David Brion Davis—THE PROBLEM OF SLAVERY IN THE AGE OF REVOLUTION, 1770–1823
Paul Horgan—LAMY OF SANTA FE
R. W. B. Lewis—EDITH WHARTON
Charles S. Maier—RECASTING BOURGEOIS EUROPE
Edmund S. Morgan—AMERICAN SLAVERY AMERICAN FREEDOM
Richard Pipes—RUSSIA UNDER THE OLD REGIME
Frank R. Rossiter—CHARLES IVES AND HIS AMERICA
Martin J. Sherwin—A WORLD DESTROYED

Poetry

*John Ashbery—SELF-PORTRAIT IN A CONVEX MIRROR
Richard Hugo—WHAT THOU LOVEST WELL, REMAINS AMERICAN
P. J. Laska—D. C. IMAGES
John N. Morris—THE LIFE BESIDE THIS ONE
Leonard Nathan—RETURNING YOUR CALL
George Oppen—COLLECTED POEMS
Carolyn M. Rodgers—HOW I GOT OVAH
Shirley Williams—THE PEACOCK POEMS

1977

Biography and Autobiography

*W. A. Swanberg—NORMAN THOMAS: THE LAST IDEALIST
Peter Collier & David Horowitz—THE ROCKEFELLERS
Anaïs Nin—THE DIARY OF ANAÏS NIN, VOL. VI
B. L. Reid—THE LIVES OF ROGER CASEMENT
E. B. White—LETTERS OF E. B. WHITE

Children's Literature

*Katherine Paterson—THE MASTER PUPPETEER
Milton Meltzer—NEVER TO FORGET: THE JEWS OF THE HOLOCAUST
John Ney—OX UNDER PRESSURE
Mildred D. Taylor—ROLL OF THUNDER, HEAR MY CRY
Barbara Wersba—TUNES FOR A SMALL HARMONICA

Contemporary Thought

*Bruno Bettelheim—THE USES OF ENCHANTMENT: THE MEANING AND IMPORTANCE OF FAIRY TALES
Dorothy Dinnerstein—THE MERMAID AND THE MINOTAUR
Joseph Frank—DOSTOEVSKY: THE SEEDS OF REVOLT

Ada Louise Huxtable—KICKED A BUILDING LATELY?
Rufus E. Miles, Jr.—AWAKENING FROM THE AMERICAN DREAM

Fiction

*Wallace Stegner—THE SPECTATOR BIRD
Raymond Carver—WILL YOU PLEASE BE QUIET, PLEASE?
MacDonald Harris—THE BALLOONIST
Ursula K. Le Guin—ORSINIAN TALES
Cynthia Propper Seton—A FINE ROMANCE

History

*Irving Howe—WORLD OF OUR FATHERS
Lawrence Goodwyn—DEMOCRATIC PROMISE
Linda Gordon—WOMAN'S BODY, WOMAN'S RIGHT
Richard Kluger—SIMPLE JUSTICE
Joshua C. Taylor—AMERICA AS ART

+*Judges' Statement:* Because Alex Haley's ROOTS does not accommodate itself to the category of History, but transcends that and other categories, members of the History panel were unable to name it as one of the nominees in History. They are at one, however, that its distinguished literary quality justifies according it a special citation of merit.

Poetry

*Richard Eberhart—COLLECTED POEMS, 1930–1976
Irving Feldman—LEAPING CLEAR AND OTHER POEMS
Margaret Newlin—THE SNOW FALLS UPWARD
Muriel Rukeyser—THE GATES
David Wagoner—COLLECTED POEMS, 1956–1976

Translation

*Li-Li Ch'en—MASTER TUNG'S WESTERN CHAMBER ROMANCE
Robert Fagles—AESCHYLUS'S THE ORESTIA
Gregory Rabassa—MARQUEZ'S THE AUTUMN OF THE PATRIARCH
Charles S. Singleton—DANTE'S THE DIVINE COMEDY, PARADISO: VOLS. I & II
Helen Weaver—ANTONIN ARTAUD: SELECTED WRITINGS

1978

Biography and Autobiography

*W. Jackson Bate—SAMUEL JOHNSON
James Atlas—DELMORE SCHWARTZ
Will D. Campbell—BROTHER TO A DRAGONFLY

Will Durant & Ariel Durant—A DUAL AUTOBIOGRAPHY
Frank E. Vandiver—BLACK JACK

Children's Literature

*Judith Kohl & Herbert Kohl—THE VIEW FROM THE OAK
Betty Sue Cummings—HEW AGAINST THE GRAIN
Ilse Koehn—MISCHLING, SECOND DEGREE
David McCord—ONE AT A TIME
William Steig—CALEB & KATE

Contemporary Thought

*Gloria Emerson—WINNERS & LOSERS
Kai T. Erikson—EVERYTHING IN ITS PATH
Michael Harrington—THE VAST MAJORITY
Louise Kapp Howe—PINK COLLAR WORKERS
Julian Jaynes—THE ORIGIN OF CONSCIOUSNESS IN THE BREAKDOWN OF THE
BICAMERAL MIND

Fiction

*Mary Lee Settle—BLOOD TIES
Robert Coover—THE PUBLIC BURNING
Peter De Vries—MADDER MUSIC
James Alan McPherson—ELBOW ROOM
John Sayles—UNION DUES

History

*David McCullough—THE PATH BETWEEN THE SEAS: THE CREATION OF THE
PANAMA CANAL 1870–1914
Henry Steele Commager—THE EMPIRE OF REASON
Robert J. Donovan—CONFLICT AND CRISIS
Joseph Kastner—A SPECIES OF ETERNITY
Fritz Stern—GOLD AND IRON

Poetry

*Howard Nemerov—THE COLLECTED POEMS OF HOWARD NEMEROV
Marvin Bell—STARS WHICH SEE, STARS WHICH DO NOT SEE
Michael S. Harper—IMAGES OF KIN
Barbara Howes—A PRIVATE SIGNAL
Charles Simic—CHARON'S COSMOLOGY

Translation

*Richard Winston & Clara Winston—UWE GEORGE'S IN THE DESERTS OF THIS
EARTH
Robert M. Adams—MACHIAVELLI'S THE PRINCE
David Lapeza—VOINOVICH'S THE IVANKIAD
Burton Watson—RYOKAN: ZEN MONK-POET OF JAPAN
William Weaver—ELSA MORANTE'S HISTORY: A NOVEL

Biography and Autobiography

*Arthur M. Schlesinger, Jr.—ROBERT KENNEDY AND HIS TIMES
Donald Hall—REMEMBERING POETS
William Manchester—AMERICAN CAESAR: DOUGLAS MACARTHUR
William M. Murphy—PRODIGAL FATHER: THE LIFE OF JOHN BUTLER YEATS
Phyllis Rose—WOMAN OF LETTERS: A LIFE OF VIRGINIA WOOLF

Children's Literature

*Katherine Paterson—THE GREAT GILLY HOPKINS
Lloyd Alexander—THE FIRST TWO LIVES OF LUKAS-KASHA
Vera Cleaver & Bill Cleaver—QUEEN OF HEARTS
Sid Fleischman—HUMBUG MOUNTAIN
Paula Fox—THE LITTLE SWINEHERD AND OTHER TALES

Contemporary Thought

*Peter Matthiessen—THE SNOW LEOPARD
Kenneth E. Boulding—STABLE PEACE
Ivan Doig—THIS HOUSE OF SKY: LANDSCAPES OF THE WESTERN MIND
Alfred Kazin—NEW YORK JEW
Meyer Schapiro—MODERN ART

Fiction

*Tim O'Brien—GOING AFTER CACCIATO
John Cheever—THE STORIES OF JOHN CHEEVER
John Irving—THE WORLD ACCORDING TO GARP
Diane Johnson—LYING LOW
David Plante—THE FAMILY

History

*Richard Beale Davis—INTELLECTUAL LIFE IN THE COLONIAL SOUTH, 1585–1763
Reinhard Bendix—KINGS OR PEOPLE
Gordon A. Craig—GERMANY, 1866–1945
John H. White, Jr.—THE AMERICAN RAILROAD PASSENGER CAR
Garry Wills—INVENTING AMERICA

Poetry

*James Merrill—MIRABELL: BOOK OF NUMBERS
Robert Hayden—AMERICAN JOURNAL
Sandra McPherson—THE YEAR OF OUR BIRTH
Philip Schultz—LIKE WINGS
May Swenson—NEW & SELECTED THINGS TAKING PLACE

Translation

*Clayton Eshleman & Jose Rubia Barcia—CESAR VALLEJO'S THE COMPLETE POSTHUMOUS POETRY
Jonathan Chaves—YUAN HUNG-TAO'S PILGRIM OF THE CLOUDS
June Guicharnaud—PIERRE-JAKES HELIAS'S THE HORSE OF PRIDE
Richard Howard—BARTHES'S A LOVER'S DISCOURSE
Reynolds Price—A PALPABLE GOD: THIRTY STORIES TRANSLATED FROM THE BIBLE

1980

Autobiography
(Hardcover)

*Lauren Bacall—LAUREN BACALL BY MYSELF
Barbara Gordon—I'M DANCING AS FAST AS I CAN
John Houseman—FRONT AND CENTER
William Saroyan—OBITUARIES

Autobiography
(Paperback)

*Malcolm Cowley—AND I WORKED AT THE WRITER'S TRADE: CHAPTERS OF LITERARY HISTORY 1918–1978

Biography
(Hardcover)

*Edmund Morris—THE RISE OF THEODORE ROOSEVELT
Millicent Bell—MARQUAND: AN AMERICAN LIFE
Leon Edel—BLOOMSBURY: A HOUSE OF LIONS
Ernest Samuels—BERNARD BERENSON: THE MAKING OF A CONNOISSEUR

Biography
(Paperback)

*A. Scott Berg—MAX PERKINS: EDITOR OF GENIUS
W. Jackson Bate—SAMUEL JOHNSON
William Manchester—AMERICAN CAESAR
Arthur M. Schlesinger, Jr.—ROBERT KENNEDY AND HIS TIMES

Children's Books
(Hardcover)

*Joan W. Blos—A GATHERING OF DAYS: A NEW ENGLAND GIRL'S JOURNAL
David Kherdian—THE ROAD FROM HOME
E. L. Konigsburg—THROWING SHADOWS
Ouida Sebestyen—WORDS BY HEART

Children's Books
(Paperback)

*Madeleine L'Engle—A SWIFTLY TILTING PLANET
    Myron Levoy—ALAN AND NAOMI
    Arnold Lobel—FROG AND TOAD ARE FRIENDS
    Katherine Paterson—THE GREAT GILLY HOPKINS
    Maurice Sendak—HIGGLETY PIGGLETY POP!: OR THERE MUST BE MORE TO
    LIFE

Current Interest
(Hardcover)

*Julia Child—JULIA CHILD AND MORE COMPANY
    Raymond Lifchez & Barbara Winslow—DESIGN FOR INDEPENDENT LIVING:
    THE ENVIRONMENT AND PHYSICALLY DISABLED PEOPLE
    Gay Gaer Luce—YOUR SECOND LIFE: VITALITY AND GROWTH IN MIDDLE AND
    LATER YEARS
    Nathan Pritikin with Patrick M. McGrady, Jr.—THE PRITIKIN PROGRAM FOR
    DIET AND EXERCISE
    Robert Ellis Smith—PRIVACY: HOW TO PROTECT WHAT'S LEFT OF IT

Current Interest
(Paperback)

*Christopher Lasch—THE CULTURE OF NARCISSISM
    Frances Wells Burck—BABYSENSE: A PRACTICAL AND SUPPORTIVE GUIDE TO
    BABY CARE
    Farallones Institute—THE INTEGRAL URBAN HOUSE: SELF-RELIANT LIVING IN
    THE CITY
    Tracy Hotchner—PREGNANCY AND CHILDBIRTH
    Calvin Trillin—ALICE, LET'S EAT

Fiction
(Hardcover)

*William Styron—SOPHIE'S CHOICE
    James Baldwin—JUST ABOVE MY HEAD
    Norman Mailer—THE EXECUTIONER'S SONG
    Philip Roth—THE GHOST WRITER
    Scott Spencer—ENDLESS LOVE

Fiction
(Paperback)

*John Irving—THE WORLD ACCORDING TO GARP
    Paul Bowles—COLLECTED STORIES
    Gail Godwin—VIOLET CLAY
    John Updike—TOO FAR TO GO

First Novel

***William Wharton**—BIRDY
Terry Davis—VISION QUEST
Stratis Haviaras—WHEN THE TREE SINGS
Philip F. O'Connor—STEALING HOME
Alan Saperstein—MOM KILLS KIDS AND SELF

General Nonfiction
(Hardcover)

***Tom Wolfe**—THE RIGHT STUFF
Frances FitzGerald—AMERICA REVISED
David Halberstam—THE POWERS THAT BE
Frederic Morton—A NERVOUS SPLENDOR: VIENNA, 1888–1889
Thomas Powers—THE MAN WHO KEPT THE SECRETS: RICHARD HELMS AND THE CIA

General Nonfiction
(Paperback)

***Peter Matthiessen**—THE SNOW LEOPARD
Sissela Bok—LYING: MORAL CHOICE IN PUBLIC AND PRIVATE LIFE
Barry Lopez—OF WOLVES AND MEN

General Reference Books
(Hardcover)

***Elder Witt, ed.**—CONGRESSIONAL QUARTERLY'S GUIDE TO THE U. S. SUPREME COURT
Frederick M. Kaplan, Julian M. Sopin & Stephen Andors—ENCYCLOPEDIA OF CHINA TODAY
Bernard Karpel—ARTS IN AMERICA: A BIBLIOGRAPHY
J. Gordon Melton—THE ENCYCLOPEDIA OF AMERICAN RELIGIONS, VOLS. I & II
Carolyn Sue Peterson, ed., & Ann D. Fenton, ed.—INDEX TO CHILDREN'S SONGS

General Reference Books
(Paperback)

***Tim Brooks & Earle Marsh**—THE COMPLETE DIRECTORY OF PRIME TIME NETWORK TV SHOWS: 1946–PRESENT
Cynthia W. Cooke, M. D., & Susan Dworkin—THE MS. GUIDE TO A WOMAN'S HEALTH
Editors of *Solar Age* magazine—THE SOLAR AGE RESOURCE BOOK
Stuart Berg Flexner—I HEAR AMERICA TALKING: AN ILLUSTRATED HISTORY OF AMERICAN WORDS AND PHRASES
Elizabeth L. Scharlatt, ed.—KIDS: DAY IN AND DAY OUT

History
(Hardcover)

*Henry A. Kissinger—THE WHITE HOUSE YEARS
Robert Dallek—FRANKLIN D. ROOSEVELT AND AMERICAN FOREIGN POLICY
George F. Kennan—DECLINE OF BISMARCK'S EUROPEAN ORDER: FRANCO-
RUSSIAN RELATIONS, 1875–1890
Frank E. Manuel & Fritzie P. Manuel—UTOPIAN THOUGHT IN THE WESTERN
WORLD
Telford Taylor—MUNICH: THE PRICE OF PEACE

History
(Paperback)

*Barbara W. Tuchman—A DISTANT MIRROR: THE CALAMITOUS 14TH CENTURY
James Lincoln Collier—THE MAKING OF JAZZ: A COMPREHENSIVE HISTORY
Daniel J. Kevles—THE PHYSICISTS: THE HISTORY OF A SCIENTIFIC
COMMUNITY IN MODERN AMERICA
Allen Weinstein—PERJURY: THE HISS-CHAMBERS CASE
Theodore H. White—IN SEARCH OF HISTORY: A PERSONAL ADVENTURE

Mystery
(Hardcover)

*John D. MacDonald—THE GREEN RIPPER
Lucille Kallen—INTRODUCING C. G. GREENFIELD
William X. Kienzle—THE ROSARY MURDERS
Arthur Maling—THE RHEINGOLD ROUTE
Lawrence Meyer—FALSE FRONT

Mystery
(Paperback)

*William F. Buckley, Jr.—STAINED GLASS
R. Wright Campbell—THE SPY WHO SAT AND WAITED
Sean Flannery—THE KREMLIN CONSPIRACY
Tony Hillerman—LISTENING WOMAN
Michael Kurland—THE INFERNAL DEVICE

Poetry

*Philip Levine—ASHES
Stanley Kunitz—THE POEMS OF STANLEY KUNITZ
David Wagoner—IN BROKEN COUNTRY

Religion/Inspiration
(Hardcover)

*Elaine Pagels—THE GNOSTIC GOSPELS
Peter L. Berger—THE HERETICAL IMPERATIVE: CONTEMPORARY POSSIBILITIES
OF RELIGIOUS AFFIRMATION

Brevard S. Childs—INTRODUCTION TO THE OLD TESTAMENT AS SCRIPTURE

Peter J. Kreeft—LOVE IS STRONGER THAN DEATH

Jack B. Rogers & Donald K. McKim—THE AUTHORITY AND INTERPRETATION OF THE BIBLE: AN HISTORICAL APPROACH

Religion/Inspiration
(Paperback)

*Sheldon Vanauken—A SEVERE MERCY

Richard Bach—ILLUSIONS: THE ADVENTURES OF A RELUCTANT MESSIAH

Catherine Marshall—THE HELPER

Science
(Hardcover)

*Douglas Hofstadter—GODEL, ESCHER, BACH: AN ETERNAL GOLDEN BRAID

Freeman Dyson—DISTURBING THE UNIVERSE

Douglas Faulkner & Richard Chesher—LIVING CORALS

Bernd Heinrich—BUMBLEBEE ECONOMICS

Horace Freeland Judson—THE EIGHTH DAY OF CREATION: MAKERS OF THE REVOLUTION IN BIOLOGY

Science
(Paperback)

*Gary Zukav—THE DANCING WU LI MASTERS: AN OVERVIEW OF THE NEW PHYSICS

William J. Kaufmann, III—BLACK HOLES AND WARPED SPACETIME

Thomas S. Kuhn—THE ESSENTIAL TENSION: SELECTED STUDIES IN SCIENTIFIC TRADITION AND CHANGE

Anne W. Simon—THE THIN EDGE: COAST AND MAN IN CRISIS

Science Fiction
(Hardcover)

*Frederik Pohl—JEM

John Crowley—ENGINE SUMMER

Thomas M. Disch—ON WINGS OF SONG

Jerry Pournelle—JANISSARIES

Kate Wilhelm—JUNIPER TIME

Science Fiction
(Paperback)

*Walter Wangerin, Jr.—THE BOOK OF THE DUN COW

Samuel R. Delany—TALES OF NEVERYON

Vonda N. McIntyre—DREAMSNAKE

Norman Spinrad—THE STAR-SPANGLED FUTURE

John Varley—THE PERSISTENCE OF VISION

Translation

*William Arrowsmith—CESARE PAVESE'S HARD LABOR
*Jane Gary Harris & Constance Link—OSIP E. MANDELSTAM'S COMPLETE
  CRITICAL PROSE AND LETTERS
  George L. Hart, III—GEORGE HART'S POETS OF THE TAMIL ANTHOLOGIES

Western

*Louis L'Amour—BENDIGO SHAFTER
  Benjamin Capps—WOMAN CHIEF
  Loren D. Estleman—THE HIGH ROCKS
  Brian Garfield—WILD TIMES
  G. Clifton Wisler—MY BROTHER, THE WIND

1981

Autobiography/Biography
(Hardcover)

*Justin Kaplan—WALT WHITMAN
  Robert K. Massie—PETER THE GREAT
  James R. Mellow—NATHANIEL HAWTHORNE IN HIS TIMES
  Peter Stansky & William Abrahams—ORWELL: THE TRANSFORMATION
  Ronald Steel—WALTER LIPPMANN AND THE AMERICAN CENTURY

Autobiography/Biography
(Paperback)

*Deirdre Bair—SAMUEL BECKETT
  E. K. Brown—WILLA CATHER
  Leon Edel—BLOOMSBURY: A HOUSE OF LIONS
  Maureen Howard—FACTS OF LIFE
  Meryle Secrest—BEING BERNARD BERENSON

Children's Books, Fiction
(Hardcover)

*Betsy Byars—THE NIGHT SWIMMERS
  Paula Fox—A PLACE APART
  Katherine Paterson—JACOB HAVE I LOVED
  Ouida Sebestyen—FAR FROM HOME
  Jan Slepian—THE ALFRED SUMMER

Children's Books, Fiction
(Paperback)

*Beverly Cleary—RAMONA AND HER MOTHER
Lloyd Alexander—THE HIGH KING
Sue Ellen Bridgers—ALL TOGETHER NOW
S. E. Hinton—TEX
Ellen Raskin—THE WESTING GAME

Children's Books, Nonfiction
(Hardcover)

*Alison Cragin Herzig & Jane Lawrence Mali—OH, BOY! BABIES
Jean Fritz—WHERE DO YOU THINK YOU'RE GOING, CHRISTOPHER COLUMBUS?
William Jaspersohn—THE BALLPARK
Milton Meltzer—ALL TIME, ALL PEOPLES: A WORLD HISTORY OF SLAVERY
Peter Spier—PEOPLE

Fiction
(Hardcover)

*Wright Morris—PLAINS SONG
Shirley Hazzard—THE TRANSIT OF VENUS
William Maxwell—SO LONG, SEE YOU TOMORROW
Walker Percy—THE SECOND COMING
Eudora Welty—THE COLLECTED STORIES

Fiction
(Paperback)

*John Cheever—THE STORIES OF JOHN CHEEVER
Thomas Flanagan—THE YEAR OF THE FRENCH
Norman Mailer—THE EXECUTIONER'S SONG
Scott Spencer—ENDLESS LOVE
Herman Wouk—WAR AND REMEMBRANCE

First Novel

*Ann Arensberg—SISTER WOLF
Jean M. Auel—THE CLAN OF THE CAVE BEAR
Philip Caputo—HORN OF AFRICA
Johanna Kaplan—O MY AMERICA
Lynne Sharon Schwartz—ROUGH STRIFE

General Nonfiction
(Hardcover)

*Maxine Hong Kingston—CHINA MEN
Malcolm Cowley—THE DREAM OF THE GOLDEN MOUNTAINS
John Graves—FROM A LIMESTONE LEDGE
Victor S. Navasky—NAMING NAMES
Studs Terkel—AMERICAN DREAMS: LOST & FOUND

General Nonfiction
(Paperback)

*Jane Kramer—THE LAST COWBOY
    Joan Didion—THE WHITE ALBUM
    David Halberstam—THE POWERS THAT BE
    Dan Morgan—MERCHANTS OF GRAIN
    Paul Theroux—THE OLD PATAGONIAN EXPRESS

History
(Hardcover)

*John Boswell—CHRISTIANITY, SOCIAL TOLERANCE AND HOMOSEXUALITY
    James H. Billington—FIRE IN THE MINDS OF MEN
    Steve Ozmont—THE AGE OF REFORM, 1250–1550
    Carl E. Schorske—FIN-DE-SIÈCLE VIENNA
    Page Smith—THE SHAPING OF AMERICA

History
(Paperback)

*Leon F. Litwak—BEEN IN THE STORM SO LONG: THE AFTERMATH OF SLAVERY
    Richard Drinnon—FACING WEST
    A. Leon Higginbotham, Jr.—IN THE MATTER OF COLOR
    Telford Taylor—MUNICH: THE PRICE OF PEACE
    Howard Zinn—A PEOPLE'S HISTORY OF THE UNITED STATES

Poetry

*Lisel Mueller—THE NEED TO HOLD STILL
    Philip Booth—BEFORE SLEEP
    Isabella Gardner—THAT WAS THEN
    Mark Strand—SELECTED POEMS
    Robert Penn Warren—BEING HERE

Science
(Hardcover)

*Stephen Jay Gould—THE PANDA'S THUMB: MORE REFLECTIONS IN NATURAL
HISTORY
    Claude C. Albritton, Jr.—THE ABYSS OF TIME
    René Dubos—THE WOOING OF EARTH
    Timothy Ferris—GALAXIES
    Carl Sagan—COSMOS

Science
(Paperback)

*Lewis Thomas—THE MEDUSA AND THE SNAIL
    Carl Sagan—BROCA'S BRAIN
    Joseph Silk—THE BIG BANG
    Walter Sullivan—BLACK HOLES

Translation

*Francis Steegmuller—THE LETTERS OF GUSTAVE FLAUBERT
*John E. Woods—ARNO SCHMIDT'S EVENING EDGED IN GOLD
    Guy Davenport—ARCHILOCHOS, SAPPHO, ALKMAN: THREE LYRIC POETS OF
    THE SEVENTH CENTURY B.C.
    John Glad—VARLAM SHALAMOV'S KOLYMA TALES
    Jean Milligan—KAO MING'S THE LUTE

1982

Autobiography/Biography
(Hardcover)

*David McCullough—MORNINGS ON HORSEBACK
    Gay Wilson Allen—WALDO EMERSON
    Dumas Malone—JEFFERSON AND HIS TIME: THE SAGE OF MONTICELLO
    William S. McFeely—GRANT
    Milton Rugoff—THE BEECHERS

Autobiography/Biography
(Paperback)

*Ronald Steel—WALTER LIPPMANN AND THE AMERICAN CENTURY
    Joseph P. Lash—HELEN AND TEACHER: THE STORY OF HELEN KELLER AND
    ANNE SULLIVAN MACY
    Robert K. Massie—PETER THE GREAT
    Ted Morgan—MAUGHAM
    Ernest Samuels—BERNARD BERENSON: THE MAKING OF A CONNOISSEUR

Children's Books, Fiction
(Hardcover)

*Lloyd Alexander—WESTMARK
    Beverly Cleary—RAMONA QUIMBY, AGE 8
    Deborah Hautzig—SECOND STAR TO THE RIGHT
    Mildred D. Taylor—LET THE CIRCLE BE UNBROKEN
    Cynthia Voigt—HOMECOMING

Children's Books, Fiction
(Paperback)

*Ouida Sebestyen—WORDS BY HEART
    Lloyd Alexander—THE WIZARD IN THE TREE
    Jane Langton—THE FLEDGLING
    Katherine Paterson—JACOB HAVE I LOVED
    Katherine Paterson—THE MASTER PUPPETEER

Children's Books, Nonfiction

*Susan Bonners—A PENGUIN YEAR
Jean Fritz—TRAITOR: THE CASE OF BENEDICT ARNOLD
James Howe; Mal Warshaw, photos—THE HOSPITAL BOOK
Patricia Luber; James Wexler, photos—SEEDS: POP, STICK AND GLIDE
Melvin B. Zisfein; Robert Andrew Parker, ill.—FLIGHT: A PANORAMA OF
AVIATION

Children's Books, Picture Books
(Hardcover)

*Maurice Sendak—OUTSIDE OVER THERE
Olaf Baker; Stephen Gammell, ill.—WHERE THE BUFFALOES BEGIN
Arnold Lobel; Anita Lobel, ill.—ON MARKET STREET
Chris Van Allsburg—JUMANJI
Nancy Willard; Alice and Martin Provensen, ill.—A VISIT TO WILLIAM
BLAKE'S INN: POEMS FOR INNOCENT AND EXPERIENCED TRAVELERS

Children's Books, Picture Books
(Paperback)

*Peter Spier—NOAH'S ARK
Muriel Feelings; Tom Feelings, ill.—JAMBO MEANS HELLO: SWAHILI ALPHABET
BOOK
Alice and Martin Provensen, ill.—A PEACEABLE KINGDOM: THE SHAKER
ABCEDARIUS
William Sleator; Blair Lent, ill.—THE ANGRY MOON
Rosemary Wells—STANLEY & RHODA

Fiction
(Hardcover)

*John Updike—RABBIT IS RICH
Mark Helprin—ELLIS ISLAND AND OTHER STORIES
John Irving—THE HOTEL NEW HAMPSHIRE
Robert Stone—A FLAG FOR SUNRISE
William Wharton—DAD

Fiction
(Paperback)

*William Maxwell—SO LONG, SEE YOU TOMORROW
E. L. Doctorow—LOON LAKE
Shirley Hazzard—THE TRANSIT OF VENUS
Walker Percy—THE SECOND COMING
Anne Tyler—MORGAN'S PASSING

First Novel

*Robb Forman Dew—DALE LOVES SOPHIE TO DEATH
Celia Gittelson—SAVING GRACE
Bette Bao Lord—SPRING MOON
Leonard Michaels—THE MEN'S CLUB
Ted Mooney—EASY TRAVEL TO OTHER PLANETS

General Nonfiction
(Hardcover)

*Tracy Kidder—THE SOUL OF A NEW MACHINE
Guy Davenport—THE GEOGRAPHY OF THE IMAGINATION
James Fallows—NATIONAL DEFENSE
Janet Malcolm—PSYCHOANALYSIS: THE IMPOSSIBLE PROFESSION
Andrea Lee—RUSSIAN JOURNAL

General Nonfiction
(Paperback)

*Victor S. Navasky—NAMING NAMES
Norman Cousins—ANATOMY OF AN ILLNESS AS PERCEIVED BY THE PATIENT
Edward Hoagland—AFRICAN CALLIOPE: A JOURNEY TO THE SUDAN
Landon Y. Jones, Jr.—GREAT EXPECTATIONS: AMERICA AND THE BABY BOOM
GENERATION
Barbara Novak—NATURE AND CULTURE: AMERICAN LANDSCAPE PAINTING,
1825–1875

History
(Hardcover)

*Father Peter John Powell—PEOPLE OF THE SACRED MOUNTAIN: A HISTORY OF
THE NORTHERN CHEYENNE CHIEFS AND WARRIOR SOCIETIES, 1830–1879
Ray Huang—587, A YEAR OF NO SIGNIFICANCE: THE MING DYNASTY IN
DECLINE
Donald Neff—WARRIORS AT SUEZ: EISENHOWER TAKES AMERICA INTO THE
MIDDLE EAST
Russell F. Weigley—EISENHOWER'S LIEUTENANTS: THE CAMPAIGN OF FRANCE
AND GERMANY, 1944–45
C. Vann Woodward, ed.—MARY CHESTNUT'S CIVIL WAR

History
(Paperback)

*Robert Wohl—THE GENERATION OF 1914
Malcolm Cowley—THE DREAM OF THE GOLDEN MOUNTAINS
Robert Dallek—FRANKLIN D. ROOSEVELT AND AMERICAN FOREIGN POLICY,
1932–45
Carl N. Degler—AT ODDS: WOMEN AND THE FAMILY IN AMERICA FROM THE
REVOLUTION TO THE PRESENT
Charles Rembar—THE LAW OF THE LAND: THE EVOLUTION OF OUR LEGAL
SYSTEM

Poetry

*William Bronk—LIFE SUPPORTS: NEW AND COLLECTED POEMS
A. R. Ammons—A COAST OF TREES
John Ashbery—SHADOW TRAIN
Douglas Crase—THE REVISIONIST
Daniel Hoffman—BROTHERLY LOVE

Science
(Hardcover)

*Donald C. Johanson & Maitland A. Edey—LUCY: THE BEGINNINGS OF
HUMANKIND
Gene Bylinsky—LIFE IN DARWIN'S UNIVERSE: EVOLUTION AND THE COSMOS
Eric Chaisson—COSMIC DAWN: THE ORIGINS OF MATTER AND LIFE
Stephen Jay Gould—THE MISMEASURE OF MAN
Steven M. Stanley—THE NEW EVOLUTIONARY TIMETABLE: FOSSILS, GENES
AND THE ORIGIN OF SPECIES

Science
(Paperback)

*Fred Alan Wolf—TAKING THE QUANTUM LEAP: THE NEW PHYSICS FOR
NONSCIENTISTS
Freeman Dyson—DISTURBING THE UNIVERSE
Howard E. Gruber—DARWIN ON MAN: A PSYCHOLOGICAL STUDY OF
SCIENTIFIC CREATIVITY
Bernd Heinrich—BUMBLEBEE ECONOMICS
Guy Murchie—THE SEVEN MYSTERIES OF LIFE: AN EXPLORATION IN SCIENCE
AND PHILOSOPHY

Translation

*Robert Lyons Danly—HIGUCHI ICHIYO'S IN THE SHADE OF SPRING LEAVES
*Ian Hideo Levy—THE TEN THOUSAND LEAVES: A TRANSLATION OF THE
MAN'YOSHU, JAPAN'S PREMIER ANTHOLOGY OF CLASSICAL POETRY
W. S. DiPiero—LEOPARDI'S PENSIERI
Louis Iribarne—MILOSZ'S THE ISSA VALLEY
Miller Williams—SONNETS OF GIUSEPPE BELLI

--------------------- **1983** ---------------------

Autobiography/Biography
(Hardcover)

*Judith Thurman—ISAK DINESEN: THE LIFE OF A STORYTELLER
Russell Baker—GROWING UP
Robert A. Caro—THE PATH TO POWER: THE YEARS OF LYNDON JOHNSON

Robert J. Donovan—TUMULTUOUS YEARS: THE PRESIDENCY OF HARRY S. TRUMAN, 1949–1953

Lewis Mumford—SKETCHES FROM LIFE: THE EARLY YEARS

Autobiography/Biography (Paperback)

*James R. Mellow—NATHANIEL HAWTHORNE IN HIS TIME

Dumas Malone—JEFFERSON IN HIS TIME, VOL. VI: THE SAGE OF MONTICELLO

Paul Mariani—WILLIAM CARLOS WILLIAMS: A NEW WORLD NAKED

William S. McFeely—GRANT

Jean Strouse—ALICE JAMES: A BIOGRAPHY

Children's Books, Fiction (Hardcover)

*Jean Fritz—HOMESICK: MY OWN STORY

Lloyd Alexander—THE KESTREL

Edward Fenton—THE REFUGEE SUMMER

Virginia Hamilton—SWEET WHISPERS, BROTHER RUSH

Zibby Oneal—A FORMAL FEELING

Children's Books, Fiction (Paperback)

*Paula Fox—A PLACE APART

*Joyce Carol Thomas—MARKED BY FIRE

Judy Blume—TIGER EYES

Sue Ellen Bridgers—NOTES FOR ANOTHER LIFE

Lois Lowry—ANASTASIA AGAIN!

Children's Books, Nonfiction

*James Cross Giblin—CHIMNEY SWEEPS

Linda Grant De Pauw—SEAFARING WOMEN

Patricia Lauber—JOURNEY TO THE PLANETS

John Nance—LOBO OF THE TASADAY

Judith St. George—THE BROOKLYN BRIDGE

Children's Picture Books (Hardcover)

*Barbara Cooney—MISS RUMPHIUS

*William Steig—DOCTOR DE SOTO

Marcia Brown—SHADOW

Karla Kuskin; Marc Simont, ill.—THE PHILHARMONIC GETS DRESSED

Cynthia Rylant; Diane Goode, ill.—WHEN I WAS YOUNG IN THE MOUNTAINS

Children's Picture Books
(Paperback)

*Mary Ann Hoberman; Betty Fraser, ill.—A HOUSE IS A HOUSE FOR ME
Steven Kellogg—PINKERTON, BEHAVE!
Peter Koeppen—ROBERT FROST'S A SWINGER OF BIRCHES
Edward Marshall; James Marshall, ill.—SPACE CASE
Ellen Shire—THE BUNGLING BALLERINAS

Fiction
(Hardcover)

*Alice Walker—THE COLOR PURPLE
Gail Godwin—A MOTHER AND TWO DAUGHTERS
Bobbie Ann Mason—SHILOH AND OTHER STORIES
Paul Theroux—THE MOSQUITO COAST
Anne Tyler—DINNER AT THE HOMESICK RESTAURANT

Fiction
(Paperback)

*Eudora Welty—COLLECTED STORIES OF EUDORA WELTY
David Bradley—THE CHANEYSVILLE INCIDENT
Mary Gordon—THE COMPANY OF WOMEN
Marilynne Robinson—HOUSEKEEPING
Robert Stone—A FLAG FOR SUNRISE

First Novel

*Gloria Naylor—THE WOMEN OF BREWSTER PLACE
Gail Albert—MATTERS OF CHANCE
John M. Del Vecchio—THE THIRTEENTH VALLEY
Susanna Moore—MY OLD SWEETHEART
David Small—ALMOST FAMOUS

General Nonfiction

*Fox Butterfield—CHINA: ALIVE IN THE BITTER SEA
George F. Kennan—THE NUCLEAR DELUSION: SOVIET-AMERICAN RELATIONS
IN THE ATOMIC AGE
David McClintock—INDECENT EXPOSURE: A TRUE STORY OF HOLLYWOOD
AND WALL STREET
Jonathan Schell—THE FATE OF THE EARTH
Susan Sheehan—IS THERE NO PLACE ON EARTH FOR ME?

General Nonfiction
(Paperback)

*James Fallows—NATIONAL DEFENSE
Edwin R. Bayley—JOE MCCARTHY AND THE PRESS
Paul Fussell—ABROAD: BRITISH TRAVELING BETWEEN THE WARS

Al Santoli—EVERYTHING WE HAD: AN ORAL HISTORY OF THE VIETNAM WAR
Joanna L. Stratton—PIONEER WOMEN: VOICES FROM THE KANSAS FRONTIER

History
(Hardcover)

*Alan Brinkley—VOICES OF PROTEST: HUEY LONG, FATHER COUGHLIN AND THE GREAT DEPRESSION
Gordon A. Craig—THE GERMANS
Robert Darnton—THE LITERARY UNDERGROUND OF THE OLD REGIME
John Putnam Demos—ENTERTAINING SATAN
William H. McNeill—THE PURSUIT OF POWER: TECHNOLOGY, ARMED FORCE AND SOCIETY SINCE A.D. 1000
Bertram Wyatt-Brown—SOUTHERN HONOR

History
(Paperback)

*Frank E. Manuel & Fritzie P. Manuel—UTOPIAN THOUGHT IN THE WESTERN WORLD
George M. Fredrickson—WHITE SUPREMACY: A COMPARATIVE STUDY IN AMERICAN AND SOUTH AFRICAN HISTORY
Ray Huang—587, A YEAR OF NO SIGNIFICANCE: THE MING DYNASTY IN DECLINE
John Noble Wilford—THE MAPMAKERS

Original Paperback

*Lisa Goldstein—THE RED MAGICIAN
David P. Barash, Ph.D., & Judith Eve Lipton, M.D.—STOP NUCLEAR WAR: A HANDBOOK
Mark Green—WINNING BACK AMERICA
Ground Zero—NUCLEAR WAR
Marc Scott Zicree—THE TWILIGHT ZONE COMPANION

Poetry

*Galway Kinnell—SELECTED POEMS
*Charles Wright—COUNTRY MUSIC: SELECTED EARLY POEMS
Jack Gilbert—MONOLITHOS
Linda Pastan—PM/AM
Mona Van Duyn—LETTERS FROM A FATHER AND OTHER POEMS

Science
(Hardcover)

*Abraham Pais—"SUBTLE IS THE LORD . . .": THE SCIENCE AND LIFE OF ALBERT EINSTEIN
Philip J. Hilts—SCIENTIFIC TEMPERAMENTS: THREE LIVES IN CONTEMPORARY SCIENCE
Melvin Konner—THE TANGLED WING: BIOLOGICAL CONSTRAINTS ON THE HUMAN SPIRIT

Ernst Mayr—THE GROWTH OF BIOLOGICAL THOUGHT: DIVERSITY, EVOLUTION AND INHERITANCE

Heinz R. Pagels—COSMIC CODE: PHYSICS AS THE THE LANGUAGE OF NATURE

Science
(Paperback)

*Philip J. Davis & Reuben Hersh—THE MATHEMATICAL EXPERIENCE

Morris Kline—MATHEMATICS: THE LOSS OF CERTAINTY

Cynthia Moss—PORTRAIT IN THE WILD: ANIMAL BEHAVIOR IN THE WESTERN WORLD

Berton Roueché—THE MEDICAL DETECTIVES

G. Ledyard Stebbins—DARWIN TO DNA: MOLECULES TO HUMANITY

Translation

*Richard Howard—CHARLES BAUDELAIRE'S LES FLEURS DU MAL

Marion Faber—WOLFGANG HILDESHEIMER'S MOZART

Allen Mandelbaum—DANTE'S PURGATORIO

Philip B. Miller—AN ABYSS DEEP ENOUGH: LETTERS OF HEINRICH VON KLEIST

Richard Wilbur—RACINE'S ANDROMACHE

1984

Fiction

*Ellen Gilchrist—VICTORY OVER JAPAN: A BOOK OF STORIES

Alison Lurie—FOREIGN AFFAIRS

Philip Roth—THE ANATOMY LESSON

First Work of Fiction

*Harriet Doerr—STONES FOR IBARRA

Kem Nunn—TAPPING THE SOURCE

Padgett Powell—EDISTO

Nonfiction

*Robert V. Remini—ANDREW JACKSON & THE COURSE OF AMERICAN DEMOCRACY, 1833–1845

Howard M. Feinstein—BECOMING WILLIAM JAMES

Richard Marius—THOMAS MORE

Ernst Pawel—THE NIGHTMARE OF REASON: A LIFE OF FRANZ KAFKA

Eudora Welty—ONE WRITER'S BEGINNINGS

Fiction

*Don DeLillo—WHITE NOISE
Ursula K. Le Guin—ALWAYS COMING HOME
Hugh Nissenson—THE TREE OF LIFE

First Work of Fiction

*Bob Shacochis—EASY IN THE ISLANDS
Elizabeth Benedict—SLOW DANCING
Cecile Pineda—FACE

Nonfiction

*J. Anthony Lukas—COMMON GROUND: A TURBULENT DECADE IN THE LIVES OF
THREE AMERICAN FAMILIES
Daniel J. Kevles—IN THE NAME OF EUGENICS: GENETICS AND THE USES OF
HUMAN HEREDITY
Walter A. McDougall— . . . THE HEAVENS AND THE EARTH: A POLITICAL
HISTORY OF THE SPACE AGE

Fiction

*E. L. Doctorow—WORLD'S FAIR
Norman Rush—WHITES
Peter Taylor—A SUMMONS TO MEMPHIS

Nonfiction

*Barry Lopez—ARCTIC DREAMS
John Dower—WAR WITHOUT MERCY: RACE AND POWER IN THE PACIFIC WAR
Richard Kluger—THE PAPER: THE LIFE AND TIMES OF THE NEW YORK HERALD
TRIBUNE
Michael Reynolds—THE YOUNG HEMINGWAY
Theodore Rosengarten—TOMBEE: PORTRAIT OF A COTTON PLANTER

1987

Fiction

*Larry Heinemann—PACO'S STORY
Alice McDermott—THAT NIGHT
Toni Morrison—BELOVED
Howard Norman—THE NORTHERN LIGHTS
Philip Roth—THE COUNTERLIFE

Nonfiction

*Richard Rhodes—THE MAKING OF THE ATOM BOMB
David Herbert Donald—LOOK HOMEWARD: THE LIFE OF THOMAS WOLFE
James Gleick—CHAOS: MAKING A NEW SCIENCE
Claudia Koonz—MOTHERS IN THE FATHERLAND
Robert A. M. Stern, Gregory Gilmartin & Thomas Mellins—NEW YORK
1930: ARCHITECTURE AND URBANISM BETWEEN THE TWO WORLD WARS

1988

Fiction

*Pete Dexter—PARIS TROUT
Don DeLillo—LIBRA
Mary McGarry Morris—VANISHED
James F. Powers—WHEAT THAT SPRINGETH GREEN
Anne Tyler—BREATHING LESSONS

Nonfiction

*Neil Sheehan—A BRIGHT SHINING LIE: JOHN PAUL VANN AND AMERICA IN
VIETNAM
Eric Foner—RECONSTRUCTION: AMERICA'S UNFINISHED REVOLUTION,
1863–1877
Peter Gay—THE ENLIGHTENMENT: AN INTERPRETATION
Brenda Maddox—NORA: THE REAL LIFE OF MOLLY BLOOM
Jack McLaughlin—JEFFERSON AND MONTICELLO: THE BIOGRAPHY OF A
BUILDER

Fiction

*John Casey—SPARTINA
E. L. Doctorow—BILLY BATHGATE
Katherine Dunn—GEEK LOVE
Oscar Hijuelos—MAMBO KINGS PLAY SONGS OF LOVE
Amy Tan—THE JOY LUCK CLUB

Nonfiction

*Thomas L. Friedman—FROM BEIRUT TO JERUSALEM
Taylor Branch—PARTING THE WATERS: AMERICA IN THE KING YEARS, 1954–63
McGeorge Bundy—DANGER AND SURVIVAL: CHOICES ABOUT THE BOMB IN THE FIRST FIFTY YEARS
William Pfaff—BARBARIAN SENTIMENTS: HOW THE AMERICAN CENTURY ENDS
Marilynne Robinson—MOTHER COUNTRY: BRITAIN, THE WELFARE STATE AND NUCLEAR POLLUTION

Fiction

*Charles Johnson—MIDDLE PASSAGE
Felipe Alfau—CHROMOS
Elena Castedo—PARADISE
Jessica Hagedorn—DOGEATERS
Joyce Carol Oates—BECAUSE IT IS BITTER, AND BECAUSE IT IS MY HEART

Nonfiction

*Ron Chernow—THE HOUSE OF MORGAN: AN AMERICAN BANKING DYNASTY AND THE RISE OF MODERN FINANCE
Samuel G. Freedman—SMALL VICTORIES: THE REAL WORLD OF A TEACHER, HER STUDENTS AND THEIR HIGH SCHOOL
Roger Morris—RICHARD MILHOUS NIXON: THE RISE OF AN AMERICAN POLITICIAN
Steven Naifeh & Gregory White Smith—JACKSON POLLOCK: AN AMERICAN SAGA
T. H. Watkins—RIGHTEOUS PILGRIM: THE LIFE AND TIMES OF HAROLD L. ICKES, 1874–1952

Fiction

*Norman Rush—MATING
Louis Begley—WARTIME LIES
Stephen Dixon—FROG
Stanley Elkin—THE MACGUFFIN
Sandra Scofield—BEYOND DESERVING

Nonfiction

*Orlando Patterson—FREEDOM
E. J. Dionne, Jr.—WHY AMERICANS HATE POLITICS
Melissa Fay Greene—PRAYING FOR SHEETROCK
R. W. B. Lewis—THE JAMESES: A FAMILY NARRATIVE
Diane Wood Middlebrook—ANNE SEXTON: A BIOGRAPHY

Poetry

*Philip Levine—WHAT WORK IS
Andrew Hudgins—THE NEVER-ENDING
Linda McCarriston—EVA-MARY
Adrienne Rich—AN ATLAS OF THE DIFFICULT WORLD: POEMS 1988–1991
Marilyn Nelson Waniek—THE HOMEPLACE

Fiction

*Cormac McCarthy—ALL THE PRETTY HORSES
Dorothy Allison—BASTARD OUT OF CAROLINA
Cristina Garcia—DREAMING IN CUBAN
Edward P. Jones—LOST IN THE CITY
Robert Stone—OUTERBRIDGE REACH

Nonfiction

*Paul Monette—BECOMING A MAN: HALF A LIFE STORY
Edward L. Ayers—THE PROMISE OF THE NEW SOUTH
James Gleick—GENIUS: THE LIFE & SCIENCE OF RICHARD FEYNMAN
David McCullough—TRUMAN
Garry Wills—LINCOLN AT GETTYSBURG

Poetry

*Mary Oliver—NEW & SELECTED POEMS
    Hayden Carruth—COLLECTED SHORTER POEMS
    Louise Gluck—THE WILD IRIS
    Susan Mitchell—RAPTURE
    Gary Snyder—NO NATURE

1993

Fiction

*E. Annie Proulx—THE SHIPPING NEWS
    Amy Bloom—COME TO ME
    Thom Jones—THE PUGILIST AT REST
    Richard Powers—OPERATION WANDERING SOUL
    Bob Shacochis—SWIMMING IN THE VOLCANO

Nonfiction

*Gore Vidal—UNITED STATES: ESSAYS, 1952–1992
    William Leach—LAND OF DESIRE: MERCHANTS, POWER, AND THE RISE OF A
    NEW AMERICAN CULTURE
    David Levering Lewis—W. E. B. DU BOIS: BIOGRAPHY OF A RACE, 1868–1919
    Richard Slotkin—GUNFIGHTER NATION: THE MYTH OF THE FRONTIER IN
    TWENTIETH-CENTURY AMERICA
    Peter Svenson—BATTLEFIELD: FARMING A CIVIL WAR BATTLEGROUND

Poetry

*A. R. Ammons—GARBAGE
    Mark Doty—MY ALEXANDRIA
    Margaret Gibson—THE VIGIL: A POEM IN FOUR VOICES
    Donald Hall—THE MUSEUM OF CLEAR IDEAS
    Lawrence Raab—WHAT WE DON'T KNOW ABOUT EACH OTHER

1994

Fiction

*William Gaddis—A FROLIC OF HIS OWN
    Ellen Currie—MOSES SUPPOSES
    Richard Dooling—WHITE MAN'S GRAVE

Howard Norman—THE BIRD ARTIST
Grace Paley—THE COLLECTED STORIES

Nonfiction

*Sherwin B. Nuland—HOW WE DIE: REFLECTIONS ON LIFE'S FINAL CHAPTER
John Demos—THE UNREDEEMED CAPTIVE: A FAMILY STORY FROM EARLY
AMERICA
Jane Mayer & Jill Abramson—STRANGE JUSTICE: THE SELLING OF CLARENCE
THOMAS
John Edgar Wideman—FATHERALONG: A MEDITATION ON FATHERS, SONS,
RACE AND SOCIETY
Tobias Wolff—IN PHARAOH'S ARMY: MEMORIES OF THE LOST WAR

Poetry

*James Tate—WORSHIPFUL COMPANY OF FLETCHERS
Richard Howard—LIKE MOST REVELATIONS
Heather McHugh—HINGE & SIGN: POEMS, 1968–1993
Anne Porter—AN ALTOGETHER DIFFERENT LANGUAGE
David St. John—A STUDY FOR THE WORLD'S BODY

1995

Fiction

*Philip Roth—SABBATH'S THEATRE
Madison Smartt Bell—ALL SOULS' RISING
Edwidge Danticat—KRIK? KRAK!
Stephen Dixon—INTERSTATE
Rosario Ferré—THE HOUSE ON THE LAGOON

Nonfiction

*Tina Rosenberg—THE HAUNTED LAND: FACING EUROPE'S GHOSTS AFTER
COMMUNISM
Dennis Covington—SALVATION ON SAND MOUNTAIN: SNAKE HANDLING AND
REDEMPTION IN SOUTHERN APPALACHIA
Daniel C. Dennett—DARWIN'S DANGEROUS IDEA: EVOLUTION AND THE
MEANINGS OF LIFE
Jonathan Harr—A CIVIL ACTION
Maryanne Vollers—GHOSTS OF MISSISSIPPI: THE MURDER OF MEDGAR EVERS,
THE TRIALS OF BYRON DE LA BECKWITH, AND THE HAUNTING OF THE NEW
SOUTH

Poetry

*Stanley Kunitz—PASSING THROUGH: THE LATER POEMS, NEW & SELECTED
Barbara Howes—COLLECTED POEMS, 1945–1990
Josephine Jacobsen—IN THE CREVICE OF TIME: NEW AND COLLECTED POEMS
Donald Justice—NEW & SELECTED POEMS
Gary Soto—NEW AND SELECTED POEMS

1996

Fiction

*Andrea Barrett—SHIP FEVER AND OTHER STORIES
Ron Hansen—ATTICUS
Elizabeth McCracken—THE GIANT'S HOUSE
Steven Millhauser—MARTIN DRESSLER: THE TALE OF AN AMERICAN DREAMER
Janet Peery—THE RIVER BEYOND THE WORLD

Nonfiction

*James Carroll—AN AMERICAN REQUIEM: GOD, MY FATHER, AND THE WAR THAT
CAME BETWEEN US
Melissa Fay Greene—THE TEMPLE BOMBING
Paul Hendrickson—THE LIVING AND THE DEAD: ROBERT MCNAMARA AND
FIVE LIVES OF A LOST WAR
Cary Reich—THE LIFE OF NELSON A. ROCKEFELLER: WORLDS TO CONQUER,
1908–1958
Anne Roiphe—FRUITFUL: A REAL MOTHER IN THE MODERN WORLD

Poetry

*Hayden Carruth—SCRAMBLED EGGS & WHISKEY, POEMS, 1991–1995
Lucille Clifton—THE TERRIBLE STORIES
Robert Hass—SUN UNDER WOOD
Alicia Suskin Ostriker—THE CRACK IN EVERYTHING
Charles Simic—WALKING THE BLACK CAT

Young People's Literature

*Victor Martinez—PARROT IN THE OVEN: MI VIDA
Carolyn Coman—WHAT JAMIE SAW
Nancy Farmer—A GIRL NAMED DISASTER
Helen Kim—THE LONG SEASON OF RAIN
Han Nolan—SEND ME DOWN A MIRACLE

Fiction

*Charles Frazier—COLD MOUNTAIN
Don DeLillo—UNDERWORLD
Diane Johnson—LE DIVORCE
Ward Just—ECHO HOUSE
Cynthia Ozick—THE PUTTERMESSER PAPERS

Nonfiction

*Joseph J. Ellis—AMERICAN SPHINX: THE CHARACTER OF THOMAS JEFFERSON
David I. Kertzer—THE KIDNAPPING OF EDGARDO MORTARA
Jamaica Kincaid—MY BROTHER
Thomas Lynch—THE UNDERTAKING: LIFE STUDIES FROM THE DISMAL TRADE
Sam Tanenhaus—WHITTAKER CHAMBERS

Poetry

*William Meredith—EFFORT AT SPEECH: NEW & SELECTED POEMS
John Balaban—LOCUSTS AT THE EDGE OF SUMMER: NEW & SELECTED POEMS
Frank Bidart—DESIRE
Sarah Lindsay—PRIMATE BEHAVIOR
Marilyn Nelson—THE FIELDS OF PRAISE: NEW & SELECTED POEMS

Young People's Literature

*Han Nolan—DANCING ON THE EDGE
Brock Cole—THE FACTS SPEAK FOR THEMSELVES
Adele Griffin—SONS OF LIBERTY
Mary Ann McGuigan—WHERE YOU BELONG
Tor Seidler—MEAN MARGARET

Index

Aaron, Daniel, 1974, *31*
Abrahams, William, 1967, *19;* 1973, *29;*
 1981, *47*
Abrams, M. H., 1972, *25*
Abramson, Jill, 1994, *63*
Acheson, Dean, 1970, *23*
Adams, Leonie, 1955, *7*
Adams, Robert M., 1979, *40*
Adamson, J. H., 1974, *31*
Adelman, Howard B., 1967, *19*
Adkins, Jan, 1972, *25*
Agar, Herbert, 1953, *5*
Agee, James, 1952, *4;* 1958, *9*
Ahlstrom, S. E., 1973, *30*
Aiken, Conrad, 1953, *5;* 1954, *6*
Albert, Gail, 1983, *55*
Albritton, Claude C., Jr., 1981, *49*
Alexander, Lloyd, 1969, *21;* 1971, *24;*
 1979, *41;* 1981, *48;* 1982, *50;* 1982,
 50; 1983, *54*
Alfau, Felipe; 1990, *60*
Algren, Nelson, 1950, *3;* 1957, *8*
Allen, Frederick L., 1953, *5*
Allen, Gay Wilson, 1956, *7;* 1982, *50*
Allison, Dorothy, 1992, *61*
Allsburg, Chris Van, 1982, *51*
Ammons, A. R., 1972, *27;* 1973, *30;* 1975,
 36; 1982, *53;* 1993, *62*
Anderson, Jon, 1972, *27*
Andors, Stephen, 1980, *44*
Ardrey, Robert, 1962, *14*
Arendt, Hannah, 1952, *4;* 1959, *11;* 1969,
 21
Arensberg, Ann, 1981, *48*
Arieti, Silvano, 1973, *30;* 1975, *36*
Arlen, Michael J., 1976, *37*
Arnow, Harriet, 1955, *6*
Arrowsmith, William, 1980, *47*
Arvin, Newton, 1951, *3*
Ashbery, John, 1967, *19;* 1976, *38;* 1982,
 53
Ashton, E. B., 1972, *28*
Asimov, Isaac, 1961, *13*
Atlas, James, 1978, *39*
Atwell, Lester, 1959, *11*
Auchincloss, Louis, 1960, *11;* 1961, *13;*
 1965, *17;* 1967, *19*

Auden, W. H., 1952, *4;* 1956, *8;* 1961, *13;*
 1966, *18;* 1973, *30;* 1974, *31*
Auel, Jean M., 1981, *48*
Ayers, Edward L., 1992, *61*

Babbitt, Natalie, 1975, 35
Bacall, Lauren, 1980, *42*
Bach, Richard, 1980, *46*
Bacon, Helen H., 1974, *34*
Bagg, Robert, 1962, *14*
Bailyn, Bernard, 1975, *35*
Bair, Deirdre, 1981, *47*
Baker, Olaf, 1982, *51*
Baker, Russell, 1983, *53*
Balaban, John, 1975, *36;* 1997, *65*
Baldwin, James, 1957, *8;* 1962, *14;* 1964,
 16; 1980, *43*
Barash, David P., 1983, *56*
Barber, James D., 1973, *30*
Barbour, Ian G., 1975, *36*
Barcia, Jose Rubia, 1979, *42*
Bardach, John E., 1973, *30*
Barlow, Elizabeth, 1972, *27*
Barnes, Joseph, 1971, *25*
Barnet, Richard J., 1976, *37*
Barnett, Lincoln, 1950, *3*
Barone, Michael, 1973, *29*
Barr, Stringfellow, 1962, *14*
Barrett, Andrea, 1996, *64*
Barrett, Leonard E., 1975, *36*
Barrett, Paul, 1975, *36*
Barth, Alan, 1956, *7*
Barth, John, 1969, *21;* 1973, *29*
Barthelme, Donald, 1972, *25;* 1975, *35*
Barzun, Jacques, 1960, *12*
Basso, Hamilton, 1955, *6;* 1960, *11*
Bate, Walter Jackson, 1964, *16;* 1978, *39;*
 1980, *42*
Bayley, Edwin R., 1983, *55*
Beadle, George & Muriel, 1967, *19*
Bedient, Calvin, 1975, *34*
Beeman, Richard R., 1975, *34*
Begley, Louis, 1991, 61
Belitt, Ben, 1965, *17;* 1967, *20*
Bell, Madison Smartt, 1995, *63*
Bell, Marvin, 1978, *40*
Bell, Millicent, 1980, *42*

Bellah, Robert N., 1972, *27*
Bellow, Saul, 1954, *6;* 1957, *8;* 1960, *11;*
   1965, *17;* 1971, *24;* 1976, *37*
Bemis, Samuel F., 1957, *8*
Bendix, Reinhard, 1979, *41*
Benedict, Elizabeth, 1985, *58*
Benét, William Rose, 1952, *4*
Bengis, Ingrid, 1973, *28*
Bentley, Eric, 1965, *16*
Berg, A. Scott, 1980, *42*
Berger, Peter L., 1976, *37;* 1980, *45*
Berger, Raoul, 1975, *35*
Berle, A. A., 1960, *12*
Bernstein, Carl, 1975, *35*
Bernstein, Jeremy, 1974, *33*
Berrigan, Daniel, 1958, *10;* 1970, *23*
Berryman, John, 1965, *17;* 1969, *22;* 1973,
   30
Bettelheim, Bruno, 1977, *38*
Betts, Doris, 1974, *32*
Bidart, Frank, 1997, *65*
Billington, James H., 1967, *19;* 1981, *49*
Billington, Ray Allen, 1974, *32*
Bishop, Elizabeth, 1956, *8;* 1966, *18;* 1970,
   23
Blackmur, R. P., 1968, *20*
Blake, Peter, 1961, *13*
Block, Herbert, 1973, *29*
Bloom, Amy, 1993, *62*
Bloom, Harold, 1971, *24*
Blos, Joan W., 1980, *42*
Blume, Judy, 1983, *54*
Bly, Robert, 1968, *20*
Boer, Charles, 1972, *28*
Bogan, Louise, 1955, *7*
Bok, Sissela, 1980, *44*
Bolton, Isabel, 1953, *5*
Bonners, Susan, 1982, *51*
Boorstin, Daniel J., 1959, *11;* 1974, *32*
Booth, Philip, 1958, *10;* 1962, *14;* 1981, *49*
Boswell, John, 1981, *49*
Boulding, Kenneth E., 1970, *23;* 1979, *41*
Bowen, Catherine Drinker, 1958, *10*
Bowen, Croswell, 1960, *12*
Bowers, Edgar, 1957, *9*
Bowles, Paul, 1956, *7;* 1980, *43*
Boyer, Paul, 1975, *35*
Boyle, Kay, 1961, *13*
Braden, Anne, 1959, *11*
Bradley, David, 1983, *55*
Bragdon, H. W., 1968, *20*
Branch, Taylor, 1989, *60*
Brand, Stewart, ed., 1972, *26*
Brant, Irving, 1966,
Braudy, Leo, 1973,
Brazell, Karen, 1974, *34*
Bree, Germaine, 1973, *30*
Brentano, Robert, 1975, *35*
Bridgers, Sue Ellen, 1981, *48;* 1983, *54*
Brinkley, Alan, 1983, *56*
Brinnin, John Malcolm, 1972, *26*
Brittain, Robert, 1953, *5*

Bronk, William, 1982, *53*
Brooks, Gwendolyn, 1969, *22*
Brooks, Tim, 1980, *44*
Brooks, Van Wyck, 1953, *5;* 1955, *6*
Brower, Brock, 1973, *29*
Brown, Clarence, 1974, *31;* 1975, *36*
Brown, E. K., 1981, *47*
Brown, Harrison, 1955, *6*
Brown, Marcia, 1983, 54.
Browning, Don S., 1974, *33*
Bruce, Robert V., 1974, *31*
Brustein, Robert, 1965, *16*
Buchenholz, Bruce, 1975, *35*
Buckley, William F., Jr., 1980, *45*
Buechner, Frederick, 1972, *26*
Bundy, McGeorge, 1989, *60*
Burchard, John, 1962, *14*
Burck, Frances Wells, 1980, *43*
Burns, James MacGregor, 1957, *8;* 1971, *24*
Burnshaw, Stanley, 1953, *5*
Burrows, Edwin G., 1958, *10*
Bush-Brown, Albert, 1962, *14*
Butterfield, Fox, 1983, *55*
Byars, Betsy, 1973, *29;* 1981, *47*
Bylinsky, Gene, 1982, *53*

Calisher, Hortense, 1962, *14;* 1973, *28;*
   1976, *37*
Cameron, Eleanor, 1974, *32;* 1976, *38*
Campbell, R. Wright, 1980, *46*
Campbell, Robert, 1975, *35*
Campbell, Will D., 1978, *39*
Capote, Truman, 1952, *4*
Capps, Benjamin, 1980, *47*
Caputo, Philip, 1981, *48*
Caro, Robert A., 1975, *35;* 1983, *53*
Carroll, James, 1996, *64*
Carruth, Hayden, 1974, *33;* 1992, *62;*
   1996, *64*
Carson, Rachel, 1952, *4;* 1956, *7;* 1963, *15*
Carver, Raymond, 1977, *39*
Casey, John, 1989, *60*
Castedo, Elena, 1990, *60*
Cater, Douglass, 1960, *12*
Catton, Bruce, 1954, *6;* 1957, *8*
Cavell, Stanley, 1973, *30*
Chaisson, Eric, 1982, *53*
Chambers, Whittaker, 1953, *5*
Chambers, William, 1957, *8*
Chase, Stuart, 1957, *8*
Chaves, Jonathan, 1979, *42*
Cheever, John, 1958, *9;* 1974, *32;* 1979, *41;*
   1981, *48*
Ch'en, Li-Li, 1977, *39*
Chernow, Ron, 1990, *60*
Chesher, Richard, 1980, *46*
Child, Julia, 1980, *43*
Childress, Alice, 1974, *32*
Childs, Brevard S., 1980, *46*
Chomsky, Noam, 1972, *27*
Christian, William A., Jr., 1973, *30*
Chute, B. J., 1957, *8*

Chute, Marchette, 1960, *12*
Ciardi, John, 1956, 8; 1959, *11;* 1962, *14*
Ciszek, Walter, 1965, *17*
Clapp, Patricia, 1969, *21*
Clark, Eleanor, 1953, *5;* 1965, *16*
Cleary, Beverly, 1981, *48;* 1982, *50*
Cleaver, Bill, 1971, *24;* 1979, *41*
Cleaver, Vera, 1971, *24;* 1979, *41*
Cleaver, Vera and Bill, 1970, *22;* 1974, *32*
Clements, Bruce, 1975, *35*
Clifton, Lucille, 1996, *64*
Clive, John, 1974, *31;* 1974, *32*
Cobb, Jonathan, 1973, *29*
Cody, John, 1972, *25*
Cohen, Arthur A., 1972, *27*
Cohen, Stephen F., 1974, *31*
Coit, Margaret, 1958, *10*
Cole, Brock, 1997, *65*
Coles, Robert, 1971, *24*
Collier, Christopher, 1975, *35*
Collier, James Lincoln, 1975, *35;* 1980, *45*
Collier, Peter, 1977, *38*
Collins, Michael, 1975, *34*
Coman, Carolyn, 1996, *64*
Comini, Alessandra, 1975, *34*
Commager, Henry Steele, 1978, *40*
Commoner, Barry, 1972, *27*
Compton, Arthur H., 1957, *8*
Connell, Evan S., Jr., 1960, *11;* 1974, *33*
Conroy, Frank, 1968, *20*
Cooke, Cynthia W., 1980, *44*
Cooney, Barbara, 1983, *54*
Coover, Robert, 1978, *40*
Corso, Gregory, 1971, *24*
Cousins, Norman, 1982, *52*
Covington, Dennis, 1995, *63*
Cowley, Malcolm, 1980, *42;* 1981, *48;*
    1982, *52*
Cox, Harvey, 1974, *33*
Cozzens, James Gould, 1958, *9*
Craig, Gordon A., 1979, *41;* 1983, *56*
Crase, Douglas, 1982, *53*
Creeley, Robert, 1963, *15*
Croce, Arlene, 1973, *28*
Crocker, Lester G., 1974, *31*
Crowley, John, 1980, *46*
Cudahy, Sheila, 1975, *36*
Cuddihy, John Murray, 1975, *36*
cummings, e. e., 1955, *7;* 1959, *11*
Cummings, Betty Sue, 1978, *40*
Cunningham, J. V., 1961, *13*
Cunningham, Julia, 1974, *32*
Currie, Ellen, 1994, *62*

Dahlberg, Edward, 1965, *17*
Dallek, Robert, 1980, *45;* 1982, *52*
Dangerfield, George, 1961, *13*
Danly, Robert Lyons, 1982, *53*
Danticat, Edwidge, 1995, *63*
Danto, Arthur C., 1973, *30*
Darnton, Robert, 1983, *56*
Dasmann, R. F., 1964, *16*

d'Aulaire, Edgar, 1973, *29*
d'Aulaire, Ingri, 1973, *29*
Davenport, Guy, 1981, *50;* 1982, *52*
Davenport, Marcia, 1980, *43*
Davidson, Marshall, 1952, *4*
Davies, Peter, 1974, *32*
Davis, H. L., 1953, *5*
Davis, David Brion, 1967, *19;* 1976, *38*
Davis, Elmer, 1955, *7*
Davis, Kenneth S., 1973, *28*
Davis, Nuel Pharr, 1969, *21*
Davis, Philip J., 1983, *57*
Davis, Richard Beale, 1979, *41*
Davis, Terry, 1980, *44*
Day, Douglas, 1974, *31*
Degler, Carl N., 1972, *26;* 1982, *52*
DeJong, Meindert, 1969, *21*
Delany, Samuel R., 1980, *46*
DeLillo, Don, 1985, *58;* 1988, *59;* 1997, *65*
Del Vecchio, John M., 1983, *55*
Demos, John Putnam, 1983, *56;* 1994, *63*
Dennett, Daniel C., 1995, *63*
De Pauw, Linda Grant, 1983, *54*
De Voto, Bernard A., 1953, *5*
De Vries, Peter, 1978, *40*
Dew, Robb Forman, 1982, *52*
Dexter, Pete, 1988, *59*
Dickey, James, 1965, *17;* 1966, *18;* 1971,
    24; 1972, *25*
Didion, Joan, 1981, *49*
Diggins, John P., 1973, *30*
di Giovanni, Norman Thomas, 1975, *36*
Dinnerstein, Dorothy, 1977, *38*
Dionne, E. J., Jr., 1991, *61*
DiPiero, W. S., 1982, *53*
Disch, Thomas M., 1980, *46*
Dixon, Stephen, 1991, *61;* 1995, *63*
Dobzhansky, Theodosius, 1965, *17;* 1968,
    20; 1974, *33*
Doctorow, E. L., 1972, *26;* 1982, *51;* 1986,
    58; 1989, *60*
Doerr, Harriet, 1984, *57*
Doig, Ivan, 1979, *41*
Donald, David, 1961, *13;* 1971, *24*
Donald, David Herbert, 1987, *59*
Donleavy, J. P., 1959, *10*
Donovan, John, 1972, *25*
Donovan, Robert J., 1978, *40;* 1983, *54*
Dooling, Richard, 1994, *62*
Doolittle, Hilda (H.D.), 1958, *10;* 1962, *14*
Doty, Mark, 1993, *62*
Douglas, Ellen, 1974, *32*
Douglas, William O., 1953, *5;* 1961, *13*
Dowdey, Clifford, 1956, *7*
Dower, John, 1986, *58*
Drake, Leah B., 1957, *9*
Drinnon, Richard, 1981, *49*
Drummond, Donald F., 1963, *15*
Duberman, Martin, 1967, *19*
Dubos, René, 1962, *14;* 1969, *22;* 1981, *49*
Dugan, Alan, 1962, *14*
Duncan, Robert, 1961, *13*

Dunn, Katherine, 1989, *60*
Dunn, Richard, 1973, *30*
Dupee, F. W., 1952, *4*
Dupree, A. Hunter, 1960, *12*
Durant, Ariel, 1978, *40*
Durant, Will, 1958, *10;* 1978, *40*
Dworkin, Susan, 1980, *44*
Dyson, Freeman, 1980, *46;* 1982, *53*

Eaton, Charles E., 1957,
Eberhart, Richard, 1952, *4;* 1958, *10;* 1961,
    13; 1966, *18;* 1973, *30;* 1977, *39*
Eckstein, Gustav, 1971, *24*
Edel, Leon, 1963, *15;* 1973, *28;* 1980, *42;*
    1981, *47*
Eden, Lynn, 1973, *29*
Edey, Maitland A., 1982, *53*
Edmonds, Walter D., 1976, *37*
Edwards, Thomas R., 1972, *25*
Eiseley, Loren, 1961, *13;* 1970, *23*
Elkin, Stanley, 1972, *26;* 1974, *32;* 1991,
    61
Elliott, George P., 1962, *14*
Ellis, Joseph J., 1997, *65*
Ellison, Ralph, 1953, *5;* 1965, *17*
Ellmann, Richard, 1960, *12;* 1974, *31*
Emerson, Gloria, 1978, *40*
Etzioni, Amitai, 1974, *33*
Erikson, Erik H., 1970, *23*
Erikson, Kai T., 1978, *40*
Eshleman, Clayton, 1979, *42*
Estleman, Loren D., 1980, *47*
Eszterhas, Joe, 1975, *35*
Evans, Abbie Huston, 1962, *14*
Evans, Howard Ensign, 1964, *16*
Evans, Philip R., 1975, *34*
Everwine, Peter, 1974, *35*
Exley, Frederick, 1969, *21*

Faber, Marion, 1983, *57*
Faber, Norma, 1976, *37*
Fagles, Robert, 1977, *39*
Fallows, James, 1982, *52;* 1983, *55*
Farallones Institute, 1980, *43*
Farmer, Nancy, 1996, *64*
Farnham, Emily, 1972, *25*
Faulkner, Douglas, 1980, *46*
Faulkner, William, 1951, *3;* 1952, *4;* 1955,
    6; 1960, *11*
Fearing, Kenneth, 1957, *9*
Feelings, Muriel, 1982, *51*
Feelings, Tom, 1982, *51*
Feiler, Lily, 1973, *31*
Feinstein, Howard M., 1984, *57*
Feldman, Irving, 1966, *18;* 1977, *39*
Fenton, Edward, 1983, *54*
Fenton, Ann D., 1980, *44*
Ferguson, Charles, 1959, *11*
Ferkiss, Victor C., 1971, *24*
Ferlinghetti, Lawrence, 1970, *23*
Ferré, Rosario, 1995, *63*
Ferril, Thomas H., 1953, *5*

Ferris, Timothy, 1981, *49*
Feuer, Lewis S., 1975, *36*
Fischer, Louis, 1965, *17*
Fish, Stanley E., 1973, *28*
FitzGerald, Frances, 1973, *29;* 1980, *44*
Fitzgerald, Robert, 1957, *9;* 1972, *27*
Flanagan, Thomas, 1981, *48*
Flanner, Janet, 1966, *18*
Flannery, Sean, 1980, *45*
Fleischman, Sid, 1979, *41*
Flexner, Eleanor, 1973, *28*
Flexner, James Thomas, 1973, *28*
Flexner, Stuart Berg, 1980, *44*
Folland, H. F., 1974, *31*
Foner, Eric, 1988, *59*
Foote, Shelby, 1959, *11;* 1964, *16;* 1975, *35*
Ford, Jesse Hill, 1966, *18*
Fox, Paula, 1971, *24;* 1979, *41;* 1981, *47;*
    1983, *54*
Fox, Thomas C., 1973, *29*
Frank, Joseph, 1977, *38*
Frank, Waldo, 1952, *4*
Frankel, Charles, 1966, *18*
Fraser, Betty, 1983, *55*
Frazier, Charles, 1997, *65*
Fredrickson, George M., 1983, *56*
Freedman, Samuel G., 1990, *60*
Freeman, Douglas S., 1952, *4;* 1953, *5*
Freidel, Frank, 1957, *9;* 1974, *32*
Friar, Kimon, 1974, *34*
Friedenberg, Edgar Z., 1966, *18*
Friedman, Alan, 1973, *29*
Friedman, Lawrence M., 1974, *33*
Friedman, Myra, 1974, *31*
Friedman, Thomas L., 1989, *60*
Fritz, Jean, 1981, *48;* 1982, *51;* 1983, *54*
Fromm, Erich, 1952, *4;* 1974, *33*
Frost, Robert, 1963, *15*
Fruman, Norman, 1972, *25*
Fussell, Paul, 1976, *37;* 1983, *55*

Gaddis, William, 1976, *37;* 1994, *62*
Galbraith, John Kenneth, 1959, *11;* 1968,
    20; 1974, *32;* 1976, *37*
Gallagher, Michael, 1973, *31*
Gallagher, Thomas, 1953, *5*
Gammell, Stephen, 1982, *51*
Garcia, Cristina, 1992, *61*
Gardner, Isabella, 1956, *8;* 1962, *14;* 1981,
    49
Gardner, John, 1974, *32*
Gardner, Leonard, 1970, *23*
Garfield, Brian, 1980, *47*
Garrigue, Jean, 1965, *17*
Garvin, Philip, 1972, *27;* 1975, *36*
Gay, Peter, 1967, *19;* 1969, *21;* 1975, *34;*
    1988, *59*
Gelb, Arthur and Barbara, 1963, *15*
Genovese, Eugene D., 1975, *35*
George, Jean Craighead, 1973, *29*
Giblin, James Cross, 1983, *54*
Gibson, Margaret, 1993, *62*

Gilbert, Jack, 1983, *56*
Gilchrist, Ellen, 1984, *57*
Gill, Brendan, 1951, *3*
Gillis, John R., 1975, *35*
Gilman, Richard, 1975, *34*
Gilmartin, Gregory, 1987, *59*
Ginsberg, Allen, 1974, *33*
Giovanni, Nikki, 1973, *28*
Gittelson, Celia, 1982, *52*
Glad, John, 1981, *50*
Glass, Bentley, 1966, *18*
Glasser, Ronald J., 1972, *26*
Glazer, Nathan, 1964, *16*
Gleick, James, 1987, *59;* 1992, *61*
Gluck, Louise, 1992, *62*
Godwin, Gail, 1975, *35;* 1980, *43;* 1983, *55*
Goldbarth, Albert, 1975, *36*
Golden, Harry, 1959, *11*
Goldman, Eric, 1953, *5;* 1957, *9*
Goldman, Michael, 1973, *2*
Goldstein, Lisa, 1983, i
Goldstine, Herman H., 1973, *30*
Goode, Diane, 1983, *54*
Goodman, Paul, 1973, *28*
Goodwyn, Lawrence, 1977, *39*
Gordon, Barbara, 1980, *42*
Gordon, Caroline, 1952, *4*
Gordon, Linda, 1977, *39*
Gordon, Mary, 1983, *55*
Gornick, Vivian, 1974, *32*
Gottlieb, Elaine, 1968, *21*
Gould, Stephen Jay, 1981, *49;* 1982, *53*
Graham, Loren B., 1973, *30*
Grana, Cesar, 1972, *33*
Grau, Shirley Ann, 1956, *7*
Graves, John, 1961, *13;* 1981, *48*
Green, Mark, 1983, *56*
Greene, Bette, 1974, *32*
Greene, Melissa Fay, 1991, *61;* 1996, *64*
Gregory, Horace, 1952, *4;* 1962, *14*
Grene, Marjorie, 1974, *33*
Griffin, Adele, 1997, *65*
Grubb, Davis, 1955, *6*
Gruber, Howard E., 1975, *36;* 1982, *53*
Gruen, Erich S., 1975, *35*
Guicharnaud, June, 1979, *42*
Gunther, John, 1956, *8*
Guthrie, A. B., 1957, *8*
Guthrie, Tyrone, 1960, *12*

H. D. (Hilda Doolittle), 1958, *10;* 1962, *14*
Hacker, Louis, 1958, *10*
Hacker, Marilyn, 1975, *36*
Hagedorn, Hermann, 1955, *7*
Hagedorn, Jessica, 1990, *60*
Haggin, B. H., 1972, *25;* 1974, *31*
Haight, Gordon S., 1969, *21*
Halberstam, David, 1973, *29;* 1980, *44;* 1981, *49*
Hale, Nathan G., Jr., 1972, *27*
Haley, Alex, 1977, *40*

Hall, Donald, 1956, *8;* 1979, *41;* 1993, *62*
Halle, Louis J., 1968, *20*
Hamilton, Virginia, 1972, *26;* 1975, *35;* 1983, *54*
Hammer, Richard, 1972, *26*
Hand, Learned, 1953, *5*
Handlin, Oscar, 1952, *4*
Handlin, Oscar and Mary F., 1972, *26*
Hannah, Barry, 1973, *29*
Hansen, Ron, 1996, *64*
Harbaugh, William H., 1974, *31*
Hardin, Garrett, 1973, *30*
Hardwick, Elizabeth, 1975, *34*
Harper, Michael S., 1978, *40*
Harr, Jonathan, 1995, *63*
Harrington, Alan, 1960, *12*
Harrington, Michael, 1978, *40*
Harris, Jane Gary, 1980, *4*
Harris, MacDonald, 1977, *39*
Harris, Mark, 1958, *9;* 1960, *11*
Harris, Middleton, 1975, *35*
Hart, George L., III, 1980, *47*
Hart, Moss, 1960, *12*
Haskins, Katherine, 1957, *9*
Hass, Robert, 1996, *64*
Hautzig, Deborah, 1982, *50*
Hautzig, Esther, 1969, *21*
Haviaras, Stratis, 1980, *44*
Hawke, David Freeman, 1972, *25*
Hawkes, John, 1965, 17
Hawkins, David, 1965, *17*
Hayden, Robert, 1972, *27;* 1979, *41*
Hazo, Samuel, 1973, *30*
Hazzard, Shirley, 1971, *24;* 1981, *48;* 1982, *51*
Hecht, Anthony, 1974, *34*
Heezen, Bruce C., 1972, *27*
Heilbron, J. L., 1975, *36*
Heinemann, Larry, 1987, *59*
Heinrich, Bernd, 1980, *46;* 1982, *53*
Heller, Joseph, 1962, 14; 1975, *35*
Hellman, Lillian, 1970, 22; 1974, 31
Helprin, Mark, 1982, *51*
Hemingway, Ernest, 1953, *5*
Hendrickson, Paul, 1996, *64*
Herold, J. Christopher, 1959, *11*
Hersey, John, 1957, 8; 1960, *11;* 1961, *13*
Hersh, Reuben, 1983, *57*
Hersh, Seymour, 1973, *29*
Herzig, Alison Cragin, 1981, *48*
Higginbotham, A. Leon, Jr., 1981, *49*
Higgins, George V., 1973, *29*
Highet, Gilbert, 1958, *10*
Hijuelos, Oscar, 1989, *60*
Hillerman, Tony, 1980, *45*
Hillyer, Robert, 1953, *6*
Hilsman, Roger, 1968, *20*
Hilts, Philip J., 1983, *56*
Himmelfarb, Gertrude, 1969, *21*
Hinton, S. E., 1981, *48*
Hitrec, Joseph, 1969, 22
Hoagland, Edward, 1974, 31; 1982, *52*

Hoberman, Mary Ann, 1983, *55*
Hoffman, Daniel, 1973, 31; 1982, *52*
Hofstadter, Albert, 1972, *28*
Hofstadter, Douglas, 1980, 46
Hofstadter, Richard, 1956, 8; 1964, *16*
Holland, Isabelle, 1976, *37*
Hollander, John, 1972, *27;* 1973, *30*
Hollister, Charles D., 1972, *27*
Holmes, John, 1962, *14*
Hong, Howard & Edna, 1968, *21*
Hoopes, Townsend, 1970, *23;* 1974, *31*
Hoover, Marjorie L., 1975, *34*
Horgan, Paul, 1955, *7;* 1976, *38*
Horowitz, David, 1977, *38*
Hotchner, Tracy, 1980, *43*
Houseman, John, 1973, 29; 1980, 42
Howard, Maureen, 1981, *47*
Howard, Richard, 1970, *22;* 1971, *25;*
   1973, *31;* 1975, *36;* 1979, *42;* 1983,
   57; 1994, *63*
Howe, Irving, 1953, *5;* 1977, *39*
Howe, James, 1982, *51*
Howe, Louise Kapp, 1978, *40*
Howe, Mark deWolfe, 1958, *10*
Howes, Barbara, 1967, *19;* 1978, *40;* 1995,
   64
Huang, Ray, 1982, *52;* 1983, *56*
Hudgins, Andrew, 1991, *61*
Huggins, Nathan Irvin, 1972, *25*
Hugo, Richard, 1974, *33;* 1976, *38*
Hulme, Kathryn, 1957, *9*
Humes, H. L., 1960, *11*
Humphrey, William, 1959, *10*
Humphries, Rolfe, 1957, *9;* 1969, *22*
Hunt, John, 1957, *8*
Hunter, Kristin, 1974, *32*
Huxtable, Ada Louise, 1977, *39*

Iribarne, Louis, 1982, *53*
Irving, John, 1979, *41;* 1980, *43;* 1982, *51*

Jackson, Shirley, 1960, *11*
Jacobs, Jane, 1962, *14*
Jacobsen, Josephine, 1975, *36;* 1995, *64*
Janeway, Elizabeth, 1960, *11;* 1972, *26*
Janson, H. W., 1975, *34*
Jarrell, Randall, 1952, *4;* 1955, *6;* 1956, *8;*
   1961, *13;* 1966, *18*
Jaspersohn, William, 1981, *48*
Jauch, J. M., 1974, *33*
Jaynes, Julian, 1978, *40*
Jeffers, Robinson, 1955, *7*
Johanson, Donald C., 1982, *55*
Johnson, Charles, 1990, *60*
Johnson, Christopher H., 1975, *36*
Johnson, Diane, 1973, *29;* 1979, *41;* 1997,
   65
Jones, Carl, 1953, *5*
Jones, Edward P., 1992, *61*
Jones, Frank, 1971, *25*
Jones, Howard Mumford, 1960, *12;* 1965,
   17; 1972, *26*

Jones, James, 1952, *4;* 1960, *11*
Jones, Landon Y., Jr., 1982, *52*
Jones, Thom, 1993, *62*
Jones, Ward, 1960, *12*
Jordan, June, 1972, *26*
Jordan, Winthrop D., 1969, *21*
Josephson, Matthew, 1960, 12
Josephy, Alvin M., Jr., 1969, *21*
Judson, Horace Freeland, 1980, *46*
Just, Ward, 1997, *65*
Justice, Donald, 1961, *13;* 1974, *33;* 1995,
   64

Kael, Pauline, 1974, *31*
Kallen, Lucille, 1980, *45*
Kandel, Michael, 1975, *37*
Kantor, MacKinlay, 1956, *7*
Kaplan, Frederick M., 1980, *44*
Kaplan, Johanna, 1976, *37;* 1981, *48*
Kaplan, Justin, 1967, *19;* 1981, *47*
Karnow, Stanley, 1973, *29*
Karp, Walter, 1974, *33*
Karpel, Bernard, 1980, *44*
Kastner, Joseph, 1978, *40*
Kaufmann, William J., III, 1980, *46*
Kazin, Alfred, 1952, *4;* 1963, *15;* 1966, *18;*
   1979, *41*
Keeley, Edmund, 1973, *31*
Kelin, Isaac, 1973, *31*
Kellogg, Steven, 1983, *55*
Kempton, Murray, 1956, *8;* 1974, *32*
Kendall, Paul Murray, 1957, *9*
Kennan, George F., 1957, *8;* 1959, *11;*
   1968, *20;* 1973, *29;* 1980, *45;* 1983,
   55
Kennedy, Ellen Conroy, 1969, *22*
Kennedy, John F., 1957, *9*
Kerrigan, Anthony, 1974, *34;* 1975, *36*
Kertzer, David I., 1997, *65*
Ketcham, Ralph, 1972, *25*
Kevles, Daniel J., 1980, *45;* 1985, *58*
Kherdian, David, 1980, *42*
Kidder, Tracy, 1982, *52*
Kienzle, William X., 1980, *45*
Kim, Helen, 1996, *64*
Kim, Richard, 1965, *17*
Kincaid, Jamaica, 1997, *65*
King, Larry L., 1972, *26*
Kingston, Maxine Hong, 1981, *48*
Kinnell, Galway, 1965, *17;* 1969, *22;* 1972,
   27; 1983, 56
Kirk, Ruth, 1974, *33*
Kirkland, Edward Chase, 1966, *18*
Kirstein, Lincoln, 1974, *31;* 1976, *37*
Kissinger, Henry A., 1958, *10;* 1980, *45*
Kline, Morris, 1973, *30;* 1983, *57*
Kluger, Richard, 1977, *39;* 1986, *58*
Knowles, John, 1961, *13*
Koch, Kenneth, 1963, *15*
Koehn, Ilse, 1978, *40*
Koeppen, Peter, 1983, *55*
Kohl, Herbert, 1978, *40*

Kohl, Judith, 1978, 40
Konigsburg, E. L., 1974, 32; 1980, 42
Konner, Melvin, 1983, 56
Koonz, Claudia, 1987, 59
Kosinski, Jerzy, 1969, 21
Koster, R. M., 1973, 29
Kovell, Joel, 1972, 27
Kowal, Michael, 1974, 34
Kozol, Jonathan, 1968, 20
Kramer, Jane, 1981, 49
Kreeft, Peter J., 1980, 46
Kroll, Ernest, 1953, 5
Kronenberger, Louis, 1959, 11
Krutch, Joseph Wood, 1955, 6; 1960, 12
Kubly, Herbert, 1956, 7
Kuhn, Thomas S., 1980, 46
Kunitz, Stanley, 1980, 45; 1995, 64
Kurland, Michael, 1980, 45
Kuskin, Karla, 1983, 54
Kussi, Peter, 1975, 37

La Farge, John, 1955, 7
L'Amour, Louis, 1980, 47
Lane, Frederic C., 1974, 33
Lane, Helen R., 1970, 23; 1974, 34; 1975, 37
Langer, Lawrence L., 1976, 37
Langer, Suzanne K., 1968, 21; 1974, 33
Langland, Joseph, 1957, 9
Langton, Jane, 1982, 50
Lansing, Alfred, 1960, 12
Lapeza, David, 1979, 40
Larkin, Oliver, 1967, 19
Lasby, Clarence G., 1972, 26
Lasch, Christopher, 1980, 43
Lash, Joseph P., 1972, 25; 1973, 29; 1982, 50
Laska, P. J., 1976, 38
Lattimore, Richmond, 1958, 10; 1968, 21
Lauber, Patricia, 1983, 54
Laure, Ettagale, 1975, 35
Laure, Jason, 1975, 35
Lavender, David, 1955, 7
Laycock, George, 1974, 33
Leach, William, 1993, 62
Lee, Andrea, 1982, 52
Lee, Harper, 1961, 13
Leech, Margaret, 1960, 12
Le Guin, Ursula K., 1972, 26; 1973, 29; 1977, 39; 1985, 58
Leiss, William, 1973, 30
Lemay, Harding, 1972, 25
L'Engle, Madeleine, 1980, 43
Lent, Blair, 1982, 51
Leonard, John, 1974, 32
Leontief, Wassily W., 1967, 19
Lerman, Eleanor, 1974, 33
Levertov, Denise, 1962, 14; 1968, 20; 1970, 23; 1973, 30
Leveson, David, 1972, 27
Levine, Philip, 1980, 45; 1991, 61
Levinson, Andrew, 1975, 35

Levoy, Myron, 1980, 42
Levy, Ian Hideo, 1982, 53
Levy, Robert I., 1974, 33
Lewis, R. W. B., 1966, 18; 1976, 38; 1991, 61
Lewis, David Levering, 1993, 62
Lewis, Flora, 1959, 11
Lewis, Oscar, 1962, 14; 1965, 17; 1967, 19
Lewis, Richard S., 1975, 36
Lewy, Guenter, 1975, 36
Lifchez, Raymond, 1980, 43
Lifton, Betty Jean, 1973, 29
Lifton, Robert J., 1969, 22; 1974, 32
Lilienthal, David E., 1964, 16
Lindbergh, Anne Morrow, 1956, 8; 1957, 9
Lindsay, Sarah, 1997, 65
Link, Constance, 1980, 47
Lipset, Seymour M., 1964, 16
Lipton, Judith Eve, 1983, 56
Litwak, Leon F., 1981, 49
Lobel, Arnold, 1971, 24; 1980, 43; 1982, 51
Lobel, Anita, 1982, 51
Logan, Andy, 1971, 24
Lopez, Barry, 1986, 58; 1980, 44
Lord, Bette Bao, 1982, 52
Lorde, Audre, 1974, 33
Lott, Milton, 1955, 6
Lovejoy, David, 1973, 30
Lowell, Robert, 1960, 12; 1965, 17; 1970, 23
Lowry, Lois, 1983, 54
Lubell, Samuel, 1957, 9
Luber, Patricia, 1982, 51
Luce, Gay Gaer, 1980, 43
Lukas, J. Anthony, 1985, 58
Luria, S. E., 1974, 33
Lurie, Alison, 1984, 57
Lynch, Thomas, 1997, 65
Lyons, Peter, 1964, 16
Lytle, Andrew, 1958, 9

MacDonald, John D., 1980, 45
MacLeish, Archibald, 1953, 5; 1955, 7; 1959, 11; 1973, 30
Maddow, Ben, 1975, 35
Maddox, Brenda, 1988, 59
Maier, Charles S., 1976, 38
Mailer, Norman, 1968, 20; 1969, 21; 1969, 22; 1972, 26; 1972, 27; 1980, 43; 1981, 48
Malamud, Bernard, 1958, 9; 1959, 10; 1962, 14; 1964, 15; 1967, 19
Malcolm, Janet, 1982, 52
Mali, Jane Lawrence, 1981, 48
Maling, Arthur, 1980, 45
Malone, Dumas, 1952, 4; 1971, 24; 1982, 50; 1983, 54
Manchester, William, 1979, 41; 1980, 42
Mandelbaum, Allen, 1973, 31; 1983, 57
Manfred, Frederick, 1955, 6
Mangione, Jerre, 1973, 30

Manheim, Ralph, 1967, *20;* 1970, *23;*
  1972, *28;* 1974, *34;* 1975, *37*
Mann, Arthur, 1960, *12*
Mann, Thomas, 1952, *4*
Manuel, Frank E., 1969, *22;* 1980, *45;*
  1983, *56*
Manuel, Fritzie P., 1980, *45;* 1983, *56*
March, William, 1955, *6*
Mariani, Paul, 1983, *54*
Marius, Richard, 1984, *57*
Markfield, Wallace, 1965, *17*
Marquand, John P., 1952, *4*
Marsh, Earle, 1980, *44*
Marshall, Catherine, 1980, *46*
Marshall, Edward, 1983, *55*
Marshall, James, 1983, *55*
Martin, Peter, 1953, *5*
Martinez, Victor, 1996, *64*
Marty, Martin E., 1972, *27*
Mason, Bobbie Ann, 1983, *55*
Mason, Herbert, 1972, *28*
Massie, Robert K., 1981, *47;* 1982, *50*
Mathews, T. S., 1961, *13*
Mathews, Douglas, 1973, *29*
Matthews, Jackson, 1974, *34*
Matthiessen, Peter, 1966, *18;* 1973, *30;*
  1979, *41;* 1980, *44*
Mattingly, Garrett, 1960, *12*
Maxwell, William, 1962, *14;* 1981, *48;*
  1982, *51*
May, Rollo, 1970, *23*
Mayer, Jane, 1994, *63*
Mayer, Milton, 1956, *8*
Mayr, Ernst, 1983, *57*
Mazer, Norma Fox, 1974, *32*
McCarriston, Linda, 1991, *61*
McCarthy, Cormac, 1992, *61*
McCarthy, Mary, 1958, *10;* 1964, *15*
McClintock, David, 1983, *55*
McCord, David, 1976, *37;* 1978, *40*
McCracken, Elizabeth, 1996, *64*
McCullough, David, 1978, *40;* 1982, *50;*
  1992, *61*
McDermott, Alice, 1987, *59*
McDougall, Walter A., 1985, *58*
McFeely, William S., 1982, *50;* 1983, *54*
McGill, Ralph, 1964, *16*
McGinley, Phyllis, 1955, *7*
McGrady, Patrick M., Jr., 1980, *43*
McGuane, Thomas, 1974, *32*
McGuigan, Mary Ann, 1997, *65*
McHale, Tom, 1972, *26*
McHarg, Ian L., 1971, *24*
McHargue, Georgess, 1973, *29*
McHugh, Heather, 1994, *63*
McIntyre, Vonda N., 1980, *46*
McKim, Donald K., 1980, *46*
McKinney, H. Lewis, 1973, *31*
McLarney, William O., 1973, *30*
McLaughlin, Jack, 1988, *59*
McLoughlin, William G., 1972, *27*
McNeill, William H., 1964, *16;* 1983, *56*

McNickle, D'Arcy, 1972, *25*
McPhee, John, 1972, *27;* 1975, *36*
McPherson, James Alan, 1978, *40*
McPherson, Sandra, 1979, *41*
Mead, Margaret, 1973, *29*
Meaker, Gerald H., 1975, *36*
Mellins, Thomas, 1987, *59*
Mellow, James R., 1975, *35;* 1981, *47;*
  1983, *54*
Melton, J. Gordon, 1980, *44*
Meltzer, Milton, 1969, *21;* 1975, *35;* 1975,
  35; 1977, *38;* 1981, *48*
Menninger, M.D., Karl, 1969, *22*
Meredith, William, 1965, *17;* 1997, *65*
Merrill, James, 1966, *18;* 1967, *19;* 1973,
  30; 1979, *41*
Merwin, W. S., 1953, *5;* 1957, *9;* 1964, *16;*
  1968, *20;* 1971, *24;* 1974, *34;* 1975,
  36
Meyer, Lawrence, 1980, *45*
Meyer, Leonard B., 1968, *20;* 1974, *31*
Meyerhoff, Barbara G., 1975, *36*
Michaels, Leonard, 1970, *23;* 1982, *52*
Middlebrook, Diane Wood, 1991, *61*
Miles, Rufus E., Jr., 1977, *39*
Milford, Nancy, 1971, *24*
Milgram, Stanley, 1975, *36*
Miller, John C., 1960, *12*
Miller, Perry, 1957, *9*
Miller, Philip B., 1983, *57*
Miller, Warren, 1960, *11*
Millhauser, Steven, 1996, *64*
Milligan, Jean, 1981, *50*
Milliken, Max F., 1958, *10*
Mills, C. Wright, 1952, *4*
Mitchell, Susan, 1992, *62*
Mitford, Jessica, 1974, *32*
Mizener, Arthur, 1952, *4*
Mohr, Nicholasa, 1976, *37*
Monette, Paul, 1992, *61*
Monjo, F. N., 1974, *32*
Mooney, Ted, 1982, *52*
Moore, Barrington, Jr., 1967, *19*
Moore, Marianne, 1952, *4;* 1957, *9;* 1967,
  19
Moore, Merrill, 1955, *7*
Moore, Susanna, 1983, *55*
Morgan, Dan, 1981, *49*
Morgan, Edmund S., 1976, *38*
Morgan, Frederick, 1973, *30*
Morgan, Ted, 1982, *50*
Morison, Samuel Eliot, 1960, *12;* 1972, *27*
Morris, Edmund, 1980, *42*
Morris, John N., 1976, *38*
Morris, Mary McGarry, 1988, *59*
Morris, Richard B., 1966, *18*
Morris, Roger, 1990, *60*
Morris, Wright, 1955, *6;* 1957, *8;* 1958, *9;*
  1961, *13;* 1981, *48*
Morrison, Toni, 1975, *35;* 1987, *59*
Morton, Frederic, 1963, *15;* 1980, *44*
Moss, Cynthia, 1983, *57*

Moss, Howard, 1958, *10;* 1972, *27*
Moynihan, Daniel P., 1964, *16*
Mueller, Lisel, 1981, *49*
Muller, Herbert, 1953, *5*
Muller, Ronald E., 1976, *37*
Mumford, Lewis, 1952, *4;* 1957, *9;* 1962, *14;* 1968, *21;* 1971, *24;* 1983, *54*
Murchie, Guy, 1982, *53*
Murphy, William M., 1979, *41*
Murray, Albert, 1973, *28*
Murray, John Courtney, 1965, *17*
Mydans, Carl, 1960, *12*
Myers, Robert Manson, 1973, *30*

Nabokov, Vladimir, 1958, *9;* 1959, *10;* 1963, *15;* 1965, *17;* 1973, *29;* 1975, *35;* 1976, *37*
Naifeh, Steven, 1990, *60*
Nance, John, 1983, *54*
Natanson, Maurice, 1974, *33*
Nathan, Leonard, 1976, *38*
Navasky, Victor S., 1972, *26;* 1981, *48;* 1982, *52*
Naylor, Gloria, 1983, *55*
Neff, Donald, 1982, *52*
Nelson, Marilyn, 1997, *65*
Nemerov, Howard, 1959, *11;* 1961, *13;* 1963, *15;* 1978, 40
Nevins, Allan, 1960, *12;* 1972, *26*
Newlin, Margaret, 1977, *39*
Ney, John, 1977, *38*
Nims, John Frederick, 1961, *13*
Nin, Ana•s, 1977, *38*
Nissenbaum, Stephen, 1975, *35*
Nissenson, Hugh, 1985, *58*
Nochlin, Linda, 1973, *28*
Nolan, Han, 1996, *64;* 1997, *65*
Norman, Howard, 1987, *59;* 1994, 63
Northrup, F. S. C., 1953, *5*
Novak, Barbara, 1982, 52
Nowell, Elizabeth, 1961, *13*
Nozick, Robert, 1975, *36*
Nunn, Kem, 1984, *57*

Oates, Joyce Carol, 1968, *20;* 1969, *21;* 1970, *23;* 1972, *26;* 1990, 60
Oberdorfer, Don, 1972, *26*
O'Brien, Robert C., 1972, *26*
O'Brien, Tim, 1979, *41*
O'Connor, Edwin, 1957, *8;* 1967, *19*
O'Connor, Flannery, 1956, *7;* 1961, *13;* 1966, *18;* 1972, *26*
O'Connor, Philip F., 1980, *44*
Ogburn, Charles, Jr., 1960, *12*
O'Gorman, Ned, 1962, *14*
O'Hara, Frank, 1972, *27*
O'Hara, John, 1956, *7;* 1959, *10*
Oliver, Mary, 1992, *62*
Oneal, Zibby, 1983, *54*
Oppen, George, 1976, *38*
Origo, Iris, 1972, *25*
Ostriker, Alicia Suskin, 1996, *64*

Overstreet, H. A., 1950, *3*
Ozick, Cynthia, 1972, *26;* 1997, *65*
Ozmont, Steve, 1981, *49*

Packard, Vance, 1958, *10;* 1960, *12*
Pagels, Elaine, 1980, *45*
Pagels, Heinz R., 1983, *57*
Pais, Abraham, 1983, *56*
Paley, Grace, 1975, *35*
Palmer, R. R., 1965, *17*
Parker, Douglass, 1968, *21*
Parker, Robert Andrew, 1982, *51*
Pastan, Linda, 1983, 56
Paterson, Katherine, 1977, *38;* 1979, *41;* 1980, *43;* 1981, *47;* 1982, *50;* 1982, *50*
Patterson, Orlando, 1991, *61*
Paulson, Ronald, 1972, *25*
Pawel, Ernst, 1984, *57*
Paxton, Robert O., 1973, *30*
Peery, Janet, 1996, *64*
Pelikan, Jaroslav, 1972, *27;* 1975, *36*
Percy, Walker, 1962, *14;* 1967, *19;* 1972, *26;* 1981, *48;* 1982, *51*
Perenyi, Eleanor, 1975, *34*
Perrin, Noel, 1970, *22*
Pessen, Edward, 1974, *33*
Peterson, Carolyn Sue, 1980, *44*
Peterson, Virginia, 1962, *14*
Petrakis, Harry, 1966, *18;* 1967, *19*
Pfaff, William, 1989, *60*
Phillips, Harlan B., 1961, *13*
Pineda, Cecile, 1985, *58*
Pipes, Richard, 1976, *38*
Pirsig, Robert M., 1975, *35*
Plante, David, 1979, *41*
Pohl, Frederik, 1980, *46*
Porter, Anne, 1994, *63*
Porter, Eliot, 1973, *30*
Porter, Katherine Anne, 1953, *5;* 1963, *15;* 1966, *18*
Potok, Chaim, 1968, 20
Potter, David M., 1969, *22*
Pottle, Frederick A., 1967, *19*
Pound, Ezra, 1957, *9*
Pournelle, Jerry, 1980, *46*
Powell, Dawn, 1963, *15*
Powell, Padgett, 1984, *57*
Powell, Peter John, 1982, *52*
Powers, J. F., 1957, 8; 1963, *15*
Powers, James F., 1988, *59*
Powers, Richard, 1993, *62*
Powers, Thomas, 1980, *44*
Powers, William T., 1974, *33*
Preston, Edna Mitchell, 1970, *22*
Price, Reynolds, 1979, *42*
Pritikin, Nathan, 1980, *43*
Proulx, E. Annie, 1993, *62*
Provensen, Alice and Martin, 1982, *51;* 1982, *51*
Pullen, John, 1958, *10*
Purdy, James, 1960, *11*

Pusey, Merlo, 1952, *4*
Pushkarev, Boris, 1964, *16*
Pynchon, Thomas, 1964, *15;* 1974, *32*

Raab, Lawrence, 1993, *62*
Rabassa, Gregory, 1967, *20;* 1977, *39*
Radley, Philippe, 1970, *23*
Rahv, Philip, 1966, *18*
Rand, Ayn, 1958, *9*
Randall, J. G., 1953, *5*
Ransom, John Crowe, 1964, *16*
Raskin, Ellen, 1981, *48*
Rawls, John, 1972, *27*
Reece, Byron H., 1953, *6*
Reed, Ishmael, 1973, *29;* 1973, *30*
Reich, Cary, 1996, *64*
Reid, B. L., 1977, *38*
Rembar, Charles, 1982, *52*
Remini, Robert V., 1984, *57*
Replansky, Naomi, 1953, *6*
Rexroth, Kenneth, 1953, *6;* 1957, *9;* 1968,
    20; 1971, *24*
Reynolds, Michael, 1986, *58*
Rhodes, Richard, 1987, *59*
Rice, Edward R., 1973, *30*
Rich, Adrienne, 1956, *8;* 1967, *19;* 1974,
    33; 1991, *61*
Richard, Adrienne, 1975, *35*
Richards, Victor, 1973, *31*
Richter, Conrad, 1961, *13*
Rieff, Philip, 1967, *19*
Robinson, Marilynne, 1983, *55;* 1989, *60*
Rodgers, Carolyn M., 1976, *38*
Roethke, Theodore, 1952, *4;* 1959, *11;*
    1965, *17*
Rogers, Jack B., 1980, *46*
Rogers, Thomas, 1969, *21;* 1973, *29*
Roiphe, Anne, 1996, *64*
Rooney, Frank, 1955, *6*
Roosevelt, Eleanor, 1950, *3*
Rose, Phyllis, 1979, *41*
Rose, Willie Lee, 1965, *17*
Rosebury, Theodore, 1971, *24*
Rosen, Charles, 1972, *25*
Rosenberg, Harold, 1973, *28*
Rosenberg, Tina, 1995, *63*
Rosenblum, Robert, 1976, *37*
Rosengarten, Theodore, 1975, *35;* 1986, *58*
Rosenthal, M. L., 1968, *20*
Rosenthal, Raymond, 1972, *28;* 1975, *37*
Ross, Nancy Wilson, 1958, *9*
Rossiter, Frank R., 1976, *38*
Rosten, Leo, 1960, *11*
Rostow, W. W., 1958, *10*
Roszak, Theodore, 1970, *23;* 1973, *30*
Roth, Philip, 1960, *11;* 1975, *35;* 1980, *43;*
    1984, *57;* 1987, *59;* 1995, *63*
Rothman, David J., 1972, *27*
Roueché, Berton, 1960, *12;* 1983, *57*
Royko, Mike, 1972, *26*
Ruether, Rosemary Radford, 1975, *36*
Rugoff, Milton, 1982, *50*

Rukeyser, Muriel, 1952, *4;* 1977, *39*
Rush, Norman, 1986, *58;* 1991, *61*
Rusk, Ralph L., 1950, *3*
Ryan, Chela Duran, 1972, *26*
Ryan, Michael, 1975, *36*
Rylant, Cynthia, 1983, *54*
Ryther, John H., 1973, *30*

Sachs, Marilyn, 1972, *26*
Sagan, Carl, 1981, *49;* 1981, *49*
St. George, Judith, 1983, *54*
St. John, David, 1994, *63*
Salamanca, J. R., 1959, *10*
Salinger, J. D., 1952, *4;* 1962, *14*
Samuels, Ernest, 1965, *17;* 1980, *42;* 1982,
    50
Sandburg, Carl, 1955, *7*
Sandeen, Ernest R., 1972, *27*
Santoli, Al, 1983, *56*
Saperstein, Alan, 1980, *44*
Saroyan, William, 1980, *42*
Sarton, May, 1953, *5;* 1956, *7;* 1958, *9;*
    1958, *10*
Sayles, John, 1978, *40*
Sayre, Nora, 1974, *32*
Schachner, Nathan, 1952, *4*
Schaeffer, Susan Fromberg, 1975, *36*
Schaller, George B., 1973, *30*
Schapiro, Meyer, 1979, *41*
Scharlatt, Elizabeth L., 1980, *44*
Schell, Jonathan, 1983, *55*
Schlesinger, Arthur M., Jr., 1960, *12;* 1961,
    13; 1966, *18;* 1974, *32;* 1979, *41;*
    1980, *42*
Schmidt, Eleanor L. M., 1973, *31*
Schneidman, Edwin S., 1974, *33*
Schoenbrun, David, 1958, *10*
Schorer, Mark, 1962, *14*
Schorske, Carl E., 1981, *49*
Schroyer, Trent, 1974, *33*
Schultz, Philip, 1979, *41*
Schurman, Franz, 1975, *35*
Schwartz, Lynne Sharon, 1981, *48*
Scofield, Sandra, 1991, *61*
Scott, Rachel, 1975, *35*
Scott, Winfield T., 1963, *15*
Seaver, Richard, 1970, *23*
Sebestyen, Ouida, 1980, *42;* 1981, *47;*
    1982, *50*
Secrest, Meryle, 1981, *47*
Seidensticker, Edward G., 1971, *25*
Seidler, Tor, 1997, *65*
Sendak, Maurice, 1980, *43;* 1982, *51*
Sennett, Richard, 1973, *29*
Seton, Anya, 1959, *10*
Seton, Cynthia Propper, 1977, *39*
Settle, Mary Lee, 1978, *40*
Sewall, Richard B., 1975, *34*
Sexton, Anne, 1961, *13;* 1963, *15*
Shacochis, Bob, 1985, *58;* 1993, *62*
Shapiro, David, 1972, *27*
Shapiro, Karl, 1959, *11*

Shapiro, Norman R., 1971, *25*
Shaplen, Robert, 1966, *18*
Shattuck, Roger, 1975, *34*
Sheaffer, Louis, 1974, *31*
Sheed, Wilfrid, 1967, *19;* 1974, *32*
Sheehan, Neil, 1988, *59*
Sheehan, Susan, 1983, *55*
Shelby, Barbara, 1968, *21*
Sheldon, Richard, 1972, *28*
Sherill, Robert, 1974, *32*
Sherrard, Phillip, 1973, *31*
Sherwin, Martin J., 1976, *38*
Shire, Ellen, 1983, *55*
Shirer, William L., 1961, *13*
Shorter, Edward, 1975, *36*
Siegel, Eli, 1958, *10*
Sigal, Clancy, 1963, *15*
Silk, Joseph, 1981, *49*
Silver, Nathan, 1968, *20*
Simic, Charles, 1978, *40;* 1996, *64*
Simmons, Ernest J., 1963, *15*
Simon, Anne W., 1980, *46*
Simon, John, 1972, *25*
Simont, Marc, 1983, *54*
Simpson, L. B., 1968, *21*
Simpson, Louis, 1964, *16;* 1966, *18;* 1973, *30*
Singer, Isaac Bashevis, 1962, *14;* 1965, *17;* 1967, *19;* 1970, *22;* 1973, *29;* 1974, *32*
Singer, Joseph, 1968, *21*
Singleton, Charles S., 1977, *39*
Skinner, B. F., 1972, *27*
Sklar, Kathryn Kish, 1974, *32*
Sleator, William, 1982, *51*
Slepian, Jan, 1981, *47*
Slotkin, Richard, 1974, *33;* 1993, *62*
Small, David, 1983, *55*
Small, George L., 1972, *27*
Smith, Aileen M., 1976, *37*
Smith, Alice Kimball, 1966, *18*
Smith, Eugene W., 1976, *37*
Smith, Gregory White, 1990, *60*
Smith, Lacey Baldwin, 1972, *25*
Smith, LeRoy, 1955, 7
Smith, Lillian, 1950, *3*
Smith, Mark, 1975, *35*
Smith, Page, 1963, *15;* 1981, *49*
Smith, Robert Ellis, 1980, *43*
Smith, William Jay, 1958, *10;* 1967, *19*
Snow, Edgar, 1959, 11
Snyder, Gary, 1992, *62*
Snyder, Zilpha Keatley, 1973, *29*
Solar Age Magazine, Editors of, 1980, *44*
Sontag, Raymond J., 1972, *27*
Sontag, Susan, 1967, *19*
Sopin, Julian M., 1980, *44*
Soto, Gary, 1995, *64*
Spacks, Patricia Meyer, 1976, *37*
Spencer, Elizabeth, 1957, *8;* 1961, *13*
Spencer, Scott, 1980, *43;* 1981, *48*
Spier, Peter, 1981, *48;* 1982, *52*

Spinrad, Norman, 1980, *46*
Stafford, Jean, 1953, *5;* 1970, *23*
Stafford, William, 1963, *15*
Stanley, Steven M., 1982, *53*
Stansky, Peter, 1967, *19;* 1973, *29;* 1981, *47*
Starbuck, George, 1961, *13*
Starr, Kevin, 1974, *31*
Stebbins, G. Ledyard, 1983, *57*
Steegmuller, Francis, 1961, *13;* 1964, *16;* 1971, *24;* 1975, *34;* 1981, *50*
Steel, Ronald, 1981, *47;* 1982, *50*
Stegner, Wallace, 1955, *7;* 1975, *34;* 1977, *39*
Steig, William, 1970, *22;* 1972, *26;* 1973, *29;* 1978, *40;* 1983, *54*
Steinbeck, John, 1953, *5;* 1955, *6*
Steinberg, Leo, 1973, *28;* 1976, *37*
Steinberg, Saul, 1974, *31*
Stern, Fritz, 1978, *40*
Stern, Robert A. M., 1987, *59*
Sterns, Raymond Phineas, 1971, *24*
Stevens, Wallace, 1951, *3;* 1955, *7;* 1958, *10*
Stevenson, Elizabeth, 1962, *14*
Stewart, George R., 1960, *12*
Stolz, Mary, 1975, *35*
Stone, Robert, 1975, *35;* 1982, *51;* 1983, *55;* 1992, *61*
Strand, Mark, 1971, *24;* 1981, *49*
Stratton, Joanna L., 1983, *56*
Straus, Erwin, 1967, *19*
Strouse, Jean, 1983, *54*
Strunk, Oliver, 1975, 34
Stuart, Jesse, 1953, 6
Styron, William, 1952, *4;* 1968, *20;* 1980, *43*
Sudhalter, Richard M., 1975, *34*
Sullivan, Walter, 1965, *17;* 1975, *36;* 1981, *49*
Sulzberger, C. L., 1971, *24*
Svenson, Peter, 1993, *62*
Swados, Harvey, 1964, *15*
Swanberg, W. A., 1977, *38*
Swenson, May, 1955, *7;* 1959, *11;* 1964, *16;* 1971, *24;* 1973, *31;* 1979, *41*

Tan, Amy, 1989, *60*
Tanenhaus, Sam, 1997, *65*
Tate, Allen, 1972, *27*
Tate, James, 1994, *63*
Taylor, Eleanor Ross, 1961, *13*
Taylor, Joshua C., 1977, *39*
Taylor, Mildred D., 1977, *38;* 1982, *50*
Taylor, Peter, 1986, *58*
Taylor, Telford, 1980, *45;* 1981, *49*
Teale, Edwin W., 1957, *9*
Temko, Allan, 1956, *8*
Terasaki, Gwen, 1958, *10*
Terkel, Studs, 1975, *35;* 1981, *48*
Terras, Victor, 1973, *31*
Thernstrom, Stephen, 1974, *33*
Theroux, Paul, 1981, *49;* 1983, *55*

Thomas, Benjamin, 1953, *5*
Thomas, Elizabeth, 1960, *12*
Thomas, Joyce Carol, 1983, 54
Thomas, Lewis, 1975, *34;* 1975, *36;* 1981, *49*
Thomas, Norman, 1955, *7*
Thompson, Earl, 1972, *26*
Thompson, John, 1969, *22*
Thompson, Lawrence, 1967, *19*
Thompson, William Irwin, 1972, *26*
Thurber, James, 1957, *8;* 1960, *12*
Thurman, Judith, 1983, *53*
Tilly, Charles, 1975, *36*
Torrence, Ridgely, 1953, *6*
Trask, Willard, 1967, *20*
Travers, Robert, 1959, *10*
Trillin, Calvin, 1980, *43*
Trilling, Lionel, 1966, *18;* 1973, *28*
Troy, William, 1968, *20*
Truman, Harry S., 1956, *8*
Trunk, Isaiah, 1973, *30*
Tuchman, Barbara W., 1963, *15;* 1972, *25;* 1980, *45*
Tucker, Robert C., 1974, *33*
Tunis, Edwin, 1970, *22*
Tunnard, Christopher, 1964, *16*
Turnbull, Colin M., 1973, *29*
Tyler, Anne, 1982, *51;* 1983, *55;* 1988, *59*

Udall, Stewart, 1964, *16*
Ujifusa, Grant, 1973, *29*
Ulam, Adam B., 1974, *32*
Unterecker, John, 1970, *22*
Updike, John, 1960, *12;* 1961, *13;* 1963, *15;* 1964, *15;* 1971, *24;* 1972, *26;* 1980, *43;* 1982, *51*
Upton, John, 1970, *23*

Vanauken, Sheldon, 1980, *46*
Vandiver, Frank E., 1978, *40*
Van Duyn, Mona, 1971, *24;* 1983, *56*
Varley, John, 1980, *46*
Veysey, Laurence, 1974, *33*
Vidal, Gore, 1970, *22;* 1974, *32;* 1993, *62*
Viereck, Peter, 1953, *6*
Vitaliano, Dorothy B., 1975, *36*
Voigt, Cynthia, 1982, *50*
Vollers, Maryanne, 1995, *63*
Vonnegut, Kurt, Jr., 1970, *23*

Wagoner, David, 1975, *36;* 1977, *39;* 1980, *45*
Wainhouse, Austryn, 1972, *28*
Wakeman, Frederick, Jr., 1974, *33*
Waldrop, Keith, 1969, *22*
Walker, Alice, 1974, *34;* 1983, *55*
Walker, Mildred, 1961, *13*
Wallant, Edward Lewis, 1962, *14*
Wangerin, Walter, Jr., 1980, *46*
Waniek, Marilyn Nelson, 1991, *61*
Ward, Aileen, 1964, *16*

Warren, Robert Penn, 1956, *7;* 1957, *9;* 1958, *10;* 1960, *12;* 1981, *49*
Warshaw, Mal, 1982, *51*
Watkins, T. H., 1990, *60*
Watkins, Glenn, 1975, *34*
Watson, Burton, 1969, *22;* 1974, *34;* 1978, *40*
Watson, Clyde, 1972, *26*
Watson, James D., 1969, *22*
Weaver, Helen, 1977, *39*
Weaver, William, 1969, *22;* 1975, *37;* 1978, *40*
Wecter, Dixon, 1953, *5*
Weigley, Russell F., 1982, *52*
Weinstein, Allen, 1980, *45*
Weintraub, Stanley, 1968, *20*
Weisheipl, James A., 1975, *34*
Weiss, Theodore, 1961, *13*
Welch, Julia, 1975, *36*
Wellek, Rene, 1966, *18*
Wells, Rosemary, 1982, *51*
Welty, Eudora, 1956, *7;* 1971, *24;* 1973, *29;* 1981, *48;* 1983, *55;* 1984, *57*
Wersba, Barbara, 1977, *38*
Werth, Arlene B., 1968, *21*
West, Jessamyn, 1952, *4*
West, Morris, 1960, *12*
Wexler, James, 1982, *51*
Whalen, Philip, 1970, *23*
Wharton, William, 1980, *44;* 1982, *51*
Wheelock, John Hall, 1957, *9;* 1962, *14*
Whelan, Richard J., 1965, *17*
White, E. B., 1955, *7;* 1971, *24;* 1977, *38*
White, John H., Jr., 1979, *41*
White, Morton, 1973, *30*
White, Theodore H., 1962, *14;* 1966, *18;* 1980, *45*
White, W. S., 1958, *10*
Whitney, Charles A., 1972, *27*
Whittemore, Reed, 1975, *36*
Whyte, William, Jr., 1957, *9*
Wicker, Tim, 1976, *37*
Wideman, John Edgar, 1994, *63*
Wiener, Norbert, 1965, *17*
Wilbur, Richard, 1957, *9;* 1972, *28;* 1983, *57*
Wilder, Alec, 1973, *28*
Wilder, Thornton, 1968, *20*
Wilford, John Noble, 1983, *56*
Wilhelm, Kate, 1980, *46*
Wilkins, Mira, 1975, *36*
Wilkins, Sophie, 1974, *34*
Wilkinson, Brenda, 1976, *37*
Willard, Beatrice E., 1973, *31*
Willard, Nancy, 1982, *51*
Williams, Joan, 1962, *14*
Williams, John, 1973, *29*
Williams, Joy, 1974, *32*
Williams, Kenneth P., 1950, *3;* 1953, *5*
Williams, Miller, 1982, *53*
Williams, Shirley, 1976, *38*

Williams, T. Harry, 1970, *23*
Williams, Thomas, 1975, *35*
Williams, William Carlos, 1950, *3;* 1952, *4;*
  1952, *4;* 1952, *4;* 1953, *5;* 1955, *7;*
  1956, *8;* 1959, *11;* 1963, *15*
Wills, Garry, 1973, *29;* 1979, *41;* 1992, *61*
Wilson, Arthur M., 1973, *28*
Wilson, Edmund, 1953, *5;* 1956, *8;* 1963,
  15
Wilson, Edward O., 1972, *27*
Winslow, Barbara, 1980, *43*
Winslow, Ola Elizabeth, 1962, *14*
Winston, Clara, 1979, *40*
Winston, Richard, 1979, *40*
Winston, Richard & Clara, 1972, *28*
Winters, Yvor, 1961, *13*
Wisler, G. Clifton, 1980, *47*
Witt, Elder, ed., 1980, *44*
Wohl, Robert, 1982, *52*
Woiwode, Larry, 1976, *37*
Wolf, Fred Alan, 1982, *53*
Wolfe, Bertram D., 1964, *16*
Wolfe, Tom, 1972, *26;* 1980, *44*
Wolff, Tobias, 1994, *63*
Wolfson, Harry Austryn, 1974, *33*

Womack, John, Jr., 1970, *23*
Wood, Gordon S., 1970, *23*
Wood, Peter H., 1975, *36*
Woods, John E., 1981, *50*
Woodward, Bob, 1975, *35*
Woodward, C. Vann, 1952, *4;* 1982, *52*
Wouk, Herman, 1952, *4;* 1956, *7;* 1981, *48*
Wright, Charles, 1974, *33;* 1983, *56*
Wright, James, 1958, *10;* 1972, *27*
Wyatt-Brown, Bertram, 1983, *56*

Yates, Richard, 1962, *14*
Young, Vernon, 1973, *28*

Zaturenska, Marya, 1955, *7*
Zemach, Harve, 1974, *32*
Zero, Ground, 1983, *56*
Zicree, Marc Scott, 1983, *56*
Ziff, Larzer, 1974, *33*
Zinn, Howard, 1981, *49*
Ziolkowski, Theodore, 1973, *30*
Zisfein, Melvin B., 1982, *51*
Zukav, Gary, 1980, *46*
Zukofsky, Louis, 1968, *20*
Zwinger, Ann H., 1973, *31*